To William Malloy,

For someone who has traveled the world & appreciates all the finer things in life.

Best Wishes,

Matt Bodus

merry Christmas 2007!
Love,
Will, Christine,
marlette, + James
Sandoval

simply
vanilla

simply
vanilla

recipes

for

everyday

use

patty elsberry | matt bolus

ELEVATE

Published by Elevate, Charleston, South Carolina.
Member of Advantage Media Group.

ELEVATE is a registered trademark and the
Elevate colophon is a trademark of Advantage Media Group, Inc.

Printed in the United States of America

First Printing: August 2006
ISBN: 978-1-60194-000-1

Most Advantage Media Group titles are available at special quantity discounts for bulk purchases for sales promotions, premiums, fundraising, and educational use. Special versions or book excerpts can also be created to fit specific needs.

For more information, please write: Special Markets, Advantage Media Group, P.O. Box 272, Charleston, SC 29402 or call 1.866.775.1696.

dedications

I wish to dedicate this book to my husband, Eric and my children: Danesa, Melissa, Christopher, Mario, and Danny for their unconditional support to this endeavor.

I also would like to thank my parents, Teodulo Vasquez and Gladis Zuniga, who has always taught me the value of inner strength, kindness, honesty, and perseverance, as well as being by biggest fans.

Quiero dedicar ese libro a mi esposo Eric y a mis hijos:
Danesa, Melissa, Christopher, Mario, y Danny por el apoyo incondicional que me han mostrado para la realización de esta obra.

También estoy muy agradecida a mis padres, Teodulo Vásquez y Gladis Zúniga, quienes me enseñaron el valor de la fuerza interior, bondad, honestidad, y perseverancia. Ellos siempre han sido mis fans mas grandes.

- Patty

I want to dedicate this book first to Kelly who has stood behind me, supported me, loved me, and put up with me though all of this, to my parents Jane and David Bolus who have always supported me and encouraged my ideas, and to all of the chefs that I have had the privelage to work for and study under and have learned so much from, I only hope that I can teach others as much.

- Matt

contents

1 : introduction :

I am a native of Honduras, Central America. I grew up in very humble circumstances. I remember watching my mother make all of the local dishes that I loved as a child. She would be cooking fresh corn tortillas and juggling three or four pots and pans on the stove at the same time. The aroma in the house when she was cooking was always fantastic! I wondered how she could keep it all straight. Her meals were always simple, but full of flavor. They smelled and tasted fantastic. I always thought my mother was the best cook in the world.

As I grew up, I learned to love cooking as well. I was never quite as handy at juggling four pans on the stove at the same time, but I learned to make pretty good meals. My first cooking lesson came from a Chinese friend. He taught me the art of simple Chinese cooking – great meats sautéed with vegetables and Chinese sauces, like oyster sauce and soy sauce. I really enjoy making good Chinese dishes.

When I came to the United States, I found a whole new world of cooking that was unknown to me. Supermarkets had shelves full of new and wonderful ingredients. The stores in my native Honduras were not as well stocked, and some ingredients were just too expensive to think about using. These new-found ingredients, along with the opportunity to learn from reading and watching TV food shows, spurred my imagination and I started to experiment more with ingredients and different dishes.

This is about the time we started Arizona Vanilla Company. Arizona Vanilla came about because I was looking for vanilla that was somewhat less expensive than $13 for two dried-up beans in the grocery store. My husband helped me find a great supplier. We decided to start a company and offer these inexpensive, quality vanilla beans to others who felt the same way. This new company launched my great desire to experiment with more and different ways to use the vanilla bean and other vanilla products.

And so this book is born. After several years in the kitchen, throwing vanilla into just about every dish I could think of, I have created a collection of vanilla dishes that we love to cook and eat. A lot of dishes didn't end up in the "Let's keep this one" pile. That is the way it is with experimentation. But we have a lot of recipes in this book that are absolutely fantastic.

Chef Matt Bolus joined me on this project because he is about as crazy about vanilla as I am! Matt is a Cordon Bleu alumnus and brings some fascinating ideas to the recipes included in this vanilla cookbook. He has been a great help in reviewing and enhancing a lot of my recipes as well as adding many dozens of his own! We had a lot of fun talking about vanilla and how to use it while we put this manuscript together.

We also want to make sure that we thank Master Chef Annemarie Huste. She has lent some wonderful dessert recipes to this body of work. Her ideas on storing and using vanilla in The Basics section are good advice for anyone to follow. You also have to try her no-cook Chocolate Mousse recipe in the Desserts section. It is simply to die for!

Vanilla is an ingredient that enhances just about any dish that contains it. Chef Matt and I would encourage anyone to experiment with vanilla. Use this cookbook as your starting place on your journey of vanilla discovery. Your results will be nothing short of amazing! So for all you vanilla lovers out there, we dedicate this book to you!

2 : vanilla tutorial :

Before I rush into how to cook with vanilla, I thought that some of you might like to learn a little bit more about my favorite spice, or is it a seasoning? Well, no matter, I have put this tutorial together so that you can gain a greater understanding of how we came to have vanilla and where it comes from. This short tutorial is not intended to be the definitive work on vanilla, but is just a short introduction so that as you start to use the recipes in this book you will know more about this wonderful seasoning. Or is it a spice? Well, I'll let greater minds than mine debate that issue. I'll just tell you about this wonder fruit of the vanilla orchid.

2.1 : a short history of vanilla :

For centuries, vanilla has been one of the most familiar flavors fundamental to Western cuisine. Commonly used to flavor desserts, beverages, milk products, and coffee, vanilla has become one of the most loved flavors of the western palate.

It is believed that the Totonaca people of Mexico were the first cultivators of vanilla during Mesoamerican times. They believed that the Gods had bestowed this exotic fruit upon them. Vanilla continues to be cultivated in the eastern portions of tropical Mexico.

In the 14th century, the Spanish conquistadors under Cortez watched Montezuma, Emperor of the Aztecs, pulverize vanilla beans, combine them with chocolate, and serve this concoction as a drink in golden goblets to his most honored guests. The Spanish caught on quickly, and by the middle of the 15th century they were importing vanilla to Europe to use as a flavor in the manufacturing of chocolate.

As European explorers and their attendant botanical recorders and collectors combed the forests of Central and South America, vanilla became more common in Europe. Europeans followed the example of the tribes in the New World and used vanilla in the production of medicine, as both a nerve stimulant and an aphrodisiac.

By the early 1800s vanilla plants were growing in botanical collections in Germany and France. Horticulturists were experimenting with conditions for its growth. From Europe it was transported to Reunion, Mauritius, and the Malagasy Republic. In the new tropical colonies, slave labor discovered that hand pollination of the flowers was necessary to produce vanilla beans.

From these points, vanilla plants were taken to Indonesia, the Seychelles, and the Comoros Islands. At approximately the same time, vanilla was introduced as a crop in Martinique and Guadeloupe in the Caribbean.

In today's world vanilla is being produced pretty much in any country that is between the Tropic of Cancer and the Tropic of Capricorn. There are many "varieties" of vanilla because each of these areas that grows vanilla has a unique flavor profile that is created due to the area in which the vanilla is grown and cured.

Which is the best? That is totally up to the user.

2.2 : the myth of vanilla :

During King Teniztli's reign, one of his wives bore him a girl of such beauty that they called her "Tzacoponziza," meaning Morningstar. To prevent anyone from enjoying her beauty, she was consecrated to the cult of Tonacayohua. But a young prince named "Xzakan-oxga" (young deer) fell in love with her although he knew that such a sacrilege was punished by beheading. One day when Morningstar came out to capture some turtle doves to offer to the goddess, he kidnapped her and ran away with her to some hidden ridges in the mountains. But they didn't get too far because the appearance of a fire breathing monster forced them to go back. When they reached the highway the priests were already expecting them and without any hesitation beheaded both Xzakan and Tzacoponziza.

With their bodies still warm, they were taken to the temple where the priests took their hearts out as an offering in atonement to the goddess and they threw the corpses from the ridge. The grass in the place of their sacrifice dried up as if their spilled blood had some malevolent spell.

Some months later a different plant began to grow in that spot so prodigiously that in a few days the place was covered by tall and thick foliage. When it reached full growth, right next to its trunk was the new sprout of a climbing orchid, growing and attaching its beautiful guides to embrace the trunk of this plant. It resembled a woman's arms with its fragile and elegant leaves. The scorching tropical sun hardly crossed the thick fronds of the plant and the soothing shade sheltered the orchid and allowed it to thrive like a bride in the arms of her lover. One morning she was covered with minimal flowers and the whole place was filled with an extraordinary aroma.

Overwhelmed by such an event, the priests and people concluded that the blood of both the prince and the princess had been transformed into the plant and the orchid. The people were even more surprised when the fragrant flowers turned into long and thin beans that when seasoned and matured let out a perfume even more penetrating. It was as if the innocent soul of Tzacoponziza had transformed in a most exquisite fragrance.

The orchid became the object of reverence and cult; it was declared a sacred plant and elevated to divine offering in every Totonac altar. And so from the blood of a princess, vanilla was born – named "xanath" (vanilla flower) in Totonac, or "tilxochitl" (black flower) in Nahuatl.

-"Leyenda de la Vainilla"
del ilustre diplomático Papanteco José J. Núñez y Domínguez

2.3 : how do we get vanilla? :

There are many species of vanilla thriving around the world; about 110 species have been catalogued since the discovery of vanilla. The plant that produces the vanilla bean is a climbing orchid. The family to which the species belongs is Orchidaceae, one of the largest families of flowering plants in the world. There are 700 genera in the family Orchidaceae and approximately 20,000 species. Orchids are best known for their beautiful flowers, which are economically valuable to the horticultural industry. However, vanilla is the only genus that has economic importance as a food source.

Vanilla is a fleshy, herbaceous climbing perennial vine. It grows to a height of from 33 to 50 feet, supporting itself on the host plant with aerial roots. Roots are produced all along the stem, opposite from the leaves. For cultivation, vanilla is trained and pruned to a height that will allow hand pollination of the flowers and subsequent harvest of the beans.

Vanilla flowers are fragrant, waxy, and large. They are pale greenish yellow in color with a short broad labellum and the upper petals are slightly smaller than the sepals. Flowers are held on long, thick rachis in groups of 20-30. Each inflorescence measures approximately four inches and usually displays three or four open flowers at a time. If flowers remain un-pollinated, they last only a day. From the state of the flowers, cultivators can judge the number of fruits that have set and can control the number of beans to a plant.

The fruit is a capsule, but in the trade of vanilla it is referred to as a "bean" or "pod". On the plant, before harvesting, the bean is pendulous, cylindrical and three-angled in shape. It reaches three inches in length and about ¾ inch in diameter at harvest size. After the beans are harvested and cured they develop their aromatic fragrance.

In Mexico and Central America bees and hummingbirds pollinate vanilla flowers in the wild. Self-pollination is impossible in other parts of the tropical world. Due to the structure and position of the stamen and the stigma and a lack of natural pollinators, hand pollination is necessary in most places where vanilla is farmed.

The most effective method used to hand pollinate vanilla flowers was discovered in 1841 and is still in use today. Individual flowers are pollinated in the early morning immediately after they open. A small stick of bamboo about the size of a toothpick is used to pollinate. The rostellum is pushed aside and pollen is spread from stamen to stigma by causing contact between the two.

2.4 : vanilla varieties :

Of the 110 varieties of vanilla, only three types are used commercially – Planifolia, Pompona, and Tahitian. Each has its own flavor, aroma, and uses. Even the same species grown and cured in different locations has different flavor profiles. In an attempt to help you sort out what's what, the following is a short discussion on some of the more common varieties.

madagascar / bourbon vanilla

Bourbon vanilla is the generic name for vanilla species planifolia. Originating in Mexico, planifolia vanilla cuttings were taken in the 1800s and grown by the French in large plantations in Reunion which was then known as the Ile de Bourbon. This explains the origins of its name. Bourbon vanilla has the familiar vanilla flavor we have come to know and love, such as that in ice cream, flavored desserts, and drinks. Madagascar bourbon is the most sought after bourbon vanilla bean and is considered the best. Madagascar has aromas of wood, oil, and leather and wide flat pods.

mexican vanilla

Vanilla is a gift of Mexico to the world. The Aztecs used vanilla: "tilxochitl" (black flower) to perfume a drink called "xocolatl" (chocolate), prepared with vanilla and cocoa for the first banquet offered to Hernando Cortez. When shown the cocoa grains and the black vanilla beans, Cortez was overwhelmed by the incredible perfume of the brown beans known as "xanath" (vanilla flower) by the Totonacs.
Mexico is no longer the largest producer of vanilla beans due to a devastating freeze in the late 1950s that destroyed most of the vanilla plants. Mexican vanilla beans are chocolate brown to black in color and their aroma is clean and delicate.

tahitian vanilla

Tahitian vanilla is the generic name for the vanilla species tahitensis. This variety originates from plant stock taken to Tahiti which probably mutated in the wild. Some believe that Tahitensis is could be a cross between the planifolia and the pompona. Now regarded as a different species, its appearance and flavor is considerably different to planifolia vanilla. Tahitian vanilla is earthly and fruity, with less natural vanillin than planifolia.

pompona (or antilles) vanilla

Pompona vanilla is grown in the Antilles and Guadeloupe in the Caribbean. The vanilla pods are considered of lower quality than either Planifolia or Tahitian. The beans tend to be smaller, around three inches, and with less vanillin than the Planifolia varieties. This species is generally used for aromatics like lotions, perfume, etc.

3 : the basics :

3.1 : how to store vanilla beans :

sealed container

The easiest way to store vanilla beans is in an airtight container. This can be a jar with a lid, Tupperware, ziplock bag, etc. The sealed container will keep the moisture in the bean, and not everywhere else. The sealed container needs to be put into a cool, dark place. This can be your cupboard or pantry, but NEVER in the refrigerator or freezer. When vanilla is placed in the refrigerator or the freezer the vanillin (the chemical essence of vanilla) will crystallize. This crystallization causes the vanilla to lose is savor, and then it becomes good for not much of anything.

vodka bottle (no, not on the rocks!)

A unique, but very useful way to store and use vanilla is to place it in a jar of cheap vodka. This method was introduced to me by Chef Annemarie Huste. Vanilla extract is made by steeping vanilla beans in grain alcohol, so what you are creating is vanilla extract in the bottle. This method will keep your vanilla beans useful for years into the future, and have the side benefit of producing a lot of vanilla extract.

Place the vanilla beans in the jar and cover them with the vodka. Don't spend a lot of money on the vodka – it won't improve the extract. What you are looking for is the alcohol that will steep all 200 plus flavor elements from the vanilla bean. I say the cheaper the better!

To store your vanilla beans in vodka:

1 quart jar with lid
1 quart of el cheapo vodka
As many vanilla beans as you want

Place the vanilla beans in the jar, then fill with the vodka. Replace the lid and store in a dark place – NOT THE REFRIGERATOR. You need to wait between 4 to 6 weeks before you use the extract that has been created and/or the vanilla beans. As you use the extract out of the jar, fill it up again with more vodka. Occasionally add more vanilla beans. This will keep a perpetual source of extract and vanilla beans to use as your work your way through your discovery of vanilla!

By the way, you probably don't want to drink vanilla extract on the rocks, because it will leave a very bad aftertaste in your mouth!

3.2 : how to use the vanilla bean :

splitting and scraping

The most common way to use the vanilla bean is the split and scrape method. This method is fairly easy to master. All you need to know is how to use a paring knife! The first thing you need to do is split the bean lengthwise using a paring knife. Then scrape the seeds.free from both sides of the bean with the edge of the knife, and add to whatever it is you are cooking. If you are cooking a sauce, add the pod to the mixture as well. When the vanilla has steeped into the sauce, strain the pod out, but DON'T THROW IT AWAY! Rinse the bean and allow it to dry at room temperature. Bury the used dry vanilla pods in your sugar for a wonderful vanilla flavored sugar. (See vanilla sugar recipe in this section.)

vanilla in the vodka

When you want to use a vanilla bean, take one out of the vodka jar. Then cut or tear a very small piece off of one end of the vanilla bean. Then squeeze from the opposite end of the vanilla bean all the way down to the cut end and all the vanilla seeds with come out and into the dish that you are preparing. Then you can replace the empty pod, cut end up, into the vodka jar to continue to create the extract.

You can also use the extract from the jar in any recipe that calls for extract. As you use the extract, replace with fresh vodka so that you always have a fresh supply of extract!

3.3 : make your own extract :

I have received a lot of questions on how to use vanilla beans. One of the best answers it to make your own extract. Extract in the stores can be expensive and you are not always sure you get the flavor that you are looking for. Making your own extract gives you the ability to use extract whenever you wish, without a lot of added expense.

The best way to make extract is by buying cheap vodka. One liter or so should do nicely. Place your vanilla beans in a tall jar large enough to hold the vanilla beans. Fill the jar with the cheap vodka. It really doesn't matter the type of vodka you use. What we are looking for here is the alcohol, not necessarily the vodka. Allow this jar to sit for at least four weeks. You will see the vodka gradually turn a dark reddish brown. This is the vanilla infusing its 200 plus flavor elements into the alcohol.

This method of extract creation works with any alcohol base that is 70 proof or above. Some like to create vanilla bourbon, vanilla whiskey, vanilla scotch, vanilla saki, vanilla rum, vanilla cognac …. well, you get the picture. Make these different types of extract, and then put the strained liquid into decorative bottles to make wonderful gift ideas!

Extract made this way can keep for years. It really has no shelf life, and as we all know, aged liquor is better then new. The same is true for vanilla extract. I know chefs who have vanilla beans in vodka that are having their fifth and sixth birthdays! You can use this extract for any recipe that calls for extract. As the extract is used, add more vodka. As you use up the vanilla beans, add more vanilla beans. This method can provide you with a perpetual supply of vanilla beans and vanilla extract!

3.4 : give your extract the taste test :

Another one of the big questions I get is how to taste vanilla extract. Pure vanilla extract is made using alcohol to seep the 200 plus flavor elements out of the vanilla beans. Not all vanilla extracts taste or smell the same. Differences can be in the use of the alcohol, the vanilla bean varieties, or blends of vanilla beans that are used. All will impart different flavor profiles to the finished extract; therefore, one pure vanilla extract is not like the next! Good vanilla extract, like all fine spirits, is better when aged.

Also, because this is an alcohol based product, you don't want to just simply stick your finger in the extract and have a taste! This will have a bitter, burning sensation, unless of course you're simply looking for a vanilla martini! There are several ways that you can taste vanilla extract and get a good idea of the flavor profile that the particular extract has.

got milk?

Add 1 teaspoon of pure vanilla extract to a six- to eight-ounce glass of fresh, cold milk. If the milk is not cold, the extract will leave a bitter taste. Completely stir the vanilla into the milk. Sip the milk slowly while moving it over the back of your mouth and tongue. This will help you to get the best sensation of the vanilla flavor.

sugar or sugar cubes

Place several drops of pure vanilla extract on a cube or teaspoon of sugar. Place in the sugar into your mouth and suck on it to allow it to melt. When this test is done with a pure vanilla extract versus an imitation vanilla, the difference is immediately noticeable. I have found that most imitation vanillas leave a bitter aftertaste.

ice cream

Using a scoop of slightly softened vanilla ice cream, (unflavored would be better but not easily obtainable unless you make it yourself) place one teaspoon of pure vanilla extract. Scoop up some of the ice cream along with the extract. The best taste receptors for vanilla are on the back of the tongue. After placing the scoop into your mouth, use your tongue to press it to the back of your mouth and allow it to dissolve.

Any of these three methods will allow you to find the extract that you like the best. They will also help you to know whether you are dealing with pure vanilla extract, or just an imitation.

3.5 : the mother sauce – simple vanilla sauce :

Most chefs will tell you that there are four basic mother sauces. Well, I believe that there should be a fifth mother sauce, vanilla sauce. Knowing how to make this sauce will allow you to create other delightful dishes. With the vanilla sauce you can create pudding, creams, and chocolate sauce, to name a few. Let your mind wander and see what delights can come from the mother of all sauces, vanilla sauce.

vanilla mother sauce
Courtesy of Master Chef Annemarie Huste

Preparation time: 5 minutes | Cook time: 30 minutes | Yield: 3 cups

Ingredients:

2 cups hot milk
1 teaspoon vanilla extract
1 cup vanilla sugar
2 egg yolks
2 eggs

Preparation:

On the top of a double broiler, combine the eggs, yolk, sugar and vanilla. Then add the hot milk and stir with a whisk over simmering water (in the bottom of the double boiler) until the sauce coats the back of a spoon. Pour into a glass container and place plastic wrap on top to prevent a skin from forming.

This sauce can be served hot or cold and can be made up to two days ahead of time.

3.6 : vanilla oil :

A great way to use the essence of vanilla is by creating your own vanilla oil. Vanilla oil is created by steeping one or two vanilla beans that have been cut and scraped and then place pod and all in oil over low heat. Below is a great simple recipe to make your own vanilla oil.

vanilla oil

Preparation time: 2 minutes | Cook time: 4-5 minutes | Yield: 2 cups

Ingredients

2 cups vegetable oil
1 vanilla bean

Preparation:

Heat the oil at low/medium. Scrape the vanilla bean and add the seeds to the oil. Whisk until the seeds are thoroughly blended with the oil. This should only take about 3 to 5 minutes. Remove from heat and pour vanilla oil into a measuring cup. Pour oil into a bottle and add the vanilla pod. Seal and store in a dark, cool place like your kitchen cupboard.

Vanilla oil can be used in vinaigrettes, oil and vinegar dressing, pancakes, waffles, or any other recipe that calls for oil. The recipes in this book will explore a lot of different uses for vanilla oils. The only limit on how to use vanilla oil is the imagination of the person using it!

3.7 : vanilla sugar and vanilla salt :

The first lesson of vanilla beans it to never, ever throw out the vanilla pod until there is absolutely, positively no aroma left in the pod. When you use the pod, rinse, let it dry, and then throw it into a container of sugar. In several weeks you will have vanilla sugar. Oh, what an aroma!

Vanilla sugar can replace regular sugar in any recipe to heighten the vanilla flavor. If you use vanilla sugar, you could use less extract or vanilla beans, but who would want to use less? As long as the pod stays in the sugar, it will continue to steep vanilla aroma and flavor into the sugar. Once the pods are removed, because vanilla is such a delicate aroma, the vanilla aroma and flavor will eventually disappear from the sugar. This process can be used with granulated sugar, confectioner sugar and brown sugar.

The same process can be used to infuse vanilla into your favorite salts. Sea salt, kosher salt, both make a wonderful base for a vanilla infused salt. Just add one to two vanilla beans to a container of your favorite salt. Allow the salt and vanilla to sit together for around two weeks in a cool, dark place, and you have a delicious vanilla salt to use with all of your favorite dishes.

Now that we have gone over the basics, it is time to have fun with vanilla. Remember: only your imagination will limit the fun and exciting dishes that you can prepare with vanilla. The recipes that follow are simply to get you started down the road of vanilla discovery. So, dig in and have some fun!

4 : juices & drinks :

Juices and drinks are a refreshing way to enjoy that wonderful aroma and taste of vanilla. An ice-cold fruit juice with vanilla can really bring out the fruity flavors and make the experience even more enjoyable.

Hot drinks are a great way to enjoy vanilla as well. What is a good cup of hot chocolate without vanilla? With hot drinks we need to worry more that the flavor does not evaporate away. Using vanilla extract in hot drinks is not a really good use of extract – hot drinks work best with ground vanilla. This pure vanilla product stays with the drink and is not carried away as the alcohol in the extract evaporates with the heat. Pure ground vanilla can be added to your ground coffee in your coffee maker. About one to two tablespoons of pure ground vanilla will give a wonderful vanilla aroma and flavor to your favorite coffee blend. The same is true of your favorite teas. Just add some ground vanilla to a teabag and allow it to steep with your favorite tea in hot water. The resulting flavor and aroma will be surprising!

Pure ground vanilla also makes a great garnish for many drinks, both hot and cold.

orange-mango juice

Preparation time: 10 minutes | Cook time: 2 minutes | Yield: 4 (8 oz. glasses)

Ingredients:

1 twelve-ounce can frozen orange juice concentrate
1 cup ripe diced mango
1 cup vanilla sugar
6 cups water
Ice cubes

Preparation:

Mix all of the ingredients in the blender. Strain the juice and serve with ice cubes.

Note: If you do not have vanilla sugar, use 1 vanilla bean and 1 cup of granulated sugar.

This drink can also be made with mango and pineapple or orange and pineapple.

vanilla lemonade

Preparation time: 3 minutes | Cook time: 2 minutes | Yield: 6-7 (8 oz. glasses)

Ingredients

3-4 juicy lemons (or limes)
1 ¼ cups vanilla sugar
2 liters of water
Ice cubes

Preparation:

Juice the lemons or limes and put into a large jar. Add the vanilla sugar and the water. Stir until the sugar is thoroughly dissolved. Add the ice cubes.

strawberry lemonade

Preparation time: 10 minutes | Cook time: 2 minutes | Yield: 4-5 (8 oz. glasses)

Ingredients:

2 cups diced strawberries
Juice of two lemons
1 cup vanilla sugar
6 cups water

Preparation:

Blend all of the ingredients and serve with ice cubes.

my kids' favorite milkshake

Preparation time: 5 minutes | Cook time: 2 minutes | Yield: 4-5 (8 oz. glasses)

Ingredients:

4 cups milk
3 tablespoons vanilla sugar
1 teaspoon vanilla extract
½ teaspoon ground cinnamon
7 ice cubes

Preparation:

Pour the milk, sugar, extract, and cinnamon into the blender. Secure the lid and turn on high. Make sure blender has the ice crusher option. Remove the little round top lid and throw in the ice cubes one at a time. Please remember to do this! Let the blender work for 1 more minute and serve immediately. It should have a very creamy consistency.

Note: If you do not have vanilla sugar, use regular sugar and 1 vanilla bean cut lengthwise and scraped. Just use the seeds to make the milkshake. Throw the pod into your sugar!

hot chocolate 101

Preparation time: 3 minutes | Cook time: 20 minutes | Yield: 2-3 cups

Ingredients:

2 cups whole milk
1/3 cup semisweet chocolate
1/8 teaspoon ground vanilla
2 teaspoons granulated sugar
1 stick whole cinnamon for garnish

Preparation:

Scald the milk with the sugar and ground vanilla stirring often. Carefully add the semisweet chocolate and stir until thoroughly dissolved. Pour it into a coffee mug and add the cinnamon stick.

eggnog

Preparation time: 2 minutes | Cook time: 25-30 minutes | Chilled time: 2-4 hours
Yield: 4 cups

Ingredients:

1 vanilla bean
1 teaspoon vanilla extract
3 eggs
4 tablespoons sugar (vanilla sugar works as well)
1 1/2 cups milk
1 1/2 cups heavy (or whipping) cream
1/2 teaspoon cinnamon
Ground mace, to taste

Preparation:

Split the vanilla bean lengthwise and scrape out the seeds. Set aside. In a bowl over simmering water, whisk together the eggs, sugar, vanilla bean seeds, and extract. Keep whisking until a ribbon is formed. Hold it at this temperature for 2-3 minutes and allow the mixture to thicken. Stir this mixture into the milk. Stir in the cinnamon.

Refrigerate this for 2 hours (or until cold). Whip the cream and add to the egg mixture. Sprinkle the top with the mace before serving.

This recipe can be spiced up a bit by using a good vanilla liqueur like Xanath. Just add to taste!

vanilla oatmeal shake

Preparation time: 3 minutes | Cook time: 5 minutes | Yield: 5 (8 oz. glasses)

Ingredients:

2 cups oats
1 cup vanilla sugar
1/8 ground cinnamon
4 cups water
ice cubes

Preparation:

Blend all of the ingredients and serve immediately. Add ice cubes and enjoy a nutritious and refreshing drink.

Note: If you want to substitute water for milk, reduce sugar to ½ cup and add 1 teaspoon vanilla extract.

vanilla cocoa mix (honduran pinol)

Preparation time: 15 minutes | Cook time: 45 minutes to 1 hour | Yield: 2 pounds

Ingredients:

2 cups rice
1 cup soy beans
1 cup whole wheat (in grain)
2 whole sticks cinnamon
1 teaspoon ground vanilla
1 cup cocoa powder
1/8 tsp ground nutmeg
1/8 tsp ground allspice
1/8 tsp ground cloves

Preparation:

Preheat a large skillet at medium heat and add the rice, soy beans, wheat grain, and cinnamon sticks to it. Roast until grains are golden brown and then remove from heat.

Allow to cool and grind together. Sift and then add the rest of the ingredients.
Add two teaspoons of vanilla-cocoa mix to a glass of water. Add sugar to taste and enjoy.

The best use for this drink is to add it to milk. Add 3 tablespoons of this mix to 3 cups of milk. Bring to a boil stirring constantly. Add sugar to taste and reduce to simmer. Remove from heat when milk has thickened.

Drink hot or cold.

Soy Milk

Preparation time: 20 minutes | Cook time: 25 minutes
Chilled time: 4 hours (or overnight) | Yield: 1 ½ liters

Ingredients:

1 pound soy beans
1 tablespoon vanilla extract
1 ½ teaspoon ground cinnamon
1 ½ cups vanilla sugar
water

Preparation:

Rinse the soybeans three times and soak in overnight in water.

Next day, put two cups of water per cup of beans in the blender. Blend and strain it in a large, deep pot. Save the crushed beans in a separate container.

Turn stove on high heat and add the vanilla extract, ground cinnamon, and the sugar. Stir constantly. When it comes to a boil, reduce to simmer. Keep stirring to prevent the milk from sticking to the bottom of the pan. Simmer for about 10 minutes and remove from heat.

Let the milk rest. When it reaches room temperature, pour into a jar. Keep in the refrigerator for at least four hours.

5 : breakfast :

Vanilla is great any time, but the dishes you can create for breakfast – pancakes, waffles, French toast, fritters. You name it, everything goes better with vanilla! In this section I have outlined a few of my family favorites. One of the staples of any breakfast is great syrup to go with those pancakes and waffles. I have included at the beginning of this Breakfast section the recipe for a simple vanilla syrup that can be used on any of the pancakes, waffles, or French toast recipes included in this book.

vanilla pancake/waffle syrup

Preparation time: 2 minutes | Cook time: 20-30 minutes | Yield: 1 cup

Ingredients:

1 cup sugar (or vanilla sugar to really kick up the flavor!)
1 tsp pure vanilla extract
1 cup water
1 vanilla bean, spilt and scraped

Preparation:

Put the water, sugar, and vanilla bean into a sauce pan. Bring to a boil. Make sure that the sugar has dissolved completely. Simmer the syrup for about 20-30 minutes and remove from heat.

Serve warm or cold.

two-minute oatmeal

Preparation time: 2 minutes | Cook time: 35 seconds | Yield: 1 cup

Ingredients

1 cup quick oatmeal
1 tablespoon sugar
1/8 teaspoon ground vanilla
1/8 teaspoon ground cinnamon
1 cup milk (separated into ½ cup each)

Preparation:

Mix all dry ingredients together with ½ cup of milk. Put into the microwave for 35 seconds. Stir and mix the other ½ cup of milk to cool the mixture. Stir again and it is ready!

Want to have some fun on a Saturday morning? Try this recipe.

campfire orange muffins

Preparation time: 15 minutes | Cook time: 20 minutes | Yield: 16 muffins

Ingredients:

1 ½ cups all purpose flour
1/3 cup vegetable oil (or vanilla oil)
1 cup orange juice
¾ cup sugar
1 teaspoon ground vanilla (or two vanilla beans)
1 teaspoon vanilla extract
3 teaspoons baking powder
3 eggs
16 orange halves (scooped empty)

Preparation:

Preheat the oven to 400 degrees. Whisk the eggs and add sugar, vanilla extract, oil, ground vanilla, and orange juice. Add flour and baking powder and stir until all ingredients are fully blended (about 2 minutes). Pour batter into orange halves. Place them in your muffin tin and bake them for 20 minutes. Remove from heat and let them cool for about 10 minutes. Serve immediately.

Note 1: If you are at a campfire, pour the batter into the orange half and cover it with the other half. Wrap in foil and cook on the grill for approximately 15 minutes per side. If using two orange halves, you will need 32 halves to use all the batter.

Note 2: If you have leftovers, discard the orange half before you put them away. Keeping the orange halves will turn your muffins bitter.

vanilla omelet rothschild

Yield: 4 servings

Ingredients:

8 whole eggs
½ cup vanilla sugar, granulated
1 Teaspoon of vanilla extract
½ cup clarified butter
½ cup Kirsch
½ cup dried apricots, diced
½ cup fresh strawberries, diced
½ cup fresh pineapple, diced

Preparation:

Preheat the oven to 400 degrees.

Soak the dried apricots in the Kirsch for about 20 minutes. (Time is not a critical issue; you want the fruit to be able to absorb the liquid and the Kirsch flavor.)

Combine the eggs, sugar, and vanilla extract in a large bowl. Whisk vigorously until the mixture is at a ribbon stage with all the sugar completely dissolved. (You are making a cold sabayon sauce which can also be used for many other recipes.)

Cover the bottom of an ovenproof pan with the sabayon (about ½ inch thick) and place in the preheated oven for 4 to 5 minutes.

Drain the apricots from the Kirsch and combine with the pineapple and strawberries. Mix well.

Remove the pan from the oven and spoon a quarter of the fruit mixture into the center of the omelet. Fold the omelet in half and slide off onto a plate.

Optional: Garnish the dish with powdered sugar, pure ground vanilla, and mint sprigs.

breakfast sausage

Preparation time: 15 minutes | Cook time: 20 minutes | Yield: 12 patties

Ingredients:

½ pound regular pork sausage
½ pound ground beef
½ teaspoon salt
1/8 teaspoon black pepper
1 tablespoon vanilla syrup
¼ teaspoon fennel seeds
1/8 teaspoon dried thyme
1 vanilla bean, split lengthwise and scraped
A pinch of cayenne pepper

Preparation:

Mix the pork sausage with the ground beef. Add salt, black pepper, vanilla syrup, fennel seeds, dried thyme, vanilla bean seeds, and cayenne.

Make meatballs and put on the grill (or in a Teflon pan) at medium heat. Let cook until golden brown. Turn to cook the other side. Remove from heat when both sides are golden brown, approximately 20 minutes.

Serve with scrambled eggs, hash browns, and fresh fruit.

grandma's sugar-free banana bread

Preparation time: 15 minutes | Cook time: 55 minutes

Ingredients:

1 1/3 cups whole wheat flour
½ cup regular Splenda
1 teaspoon baking powder
½ teaspoon baking soda
½ teaspoon salt
1 teaspoon ground cinnamon
½ cup nuts (optional)
1 ¼ cup mashed banana
1 tablespoon canola oil
1 egg
2 teaspoons vanilla extract
1/3 cup skim milk
½ teaspoon vinegar

Preparation:

Preheat oven to 350. Mix bananas, oil, eggs, and vanilla extract in a large bowl. Mix all dry ingredients in a medium bowl. Add wet ingredients and nuts to the dry ingredients. Stir until all are blended, but do not over mix. Pour batter into sprayed pan 9x5 pan and bake for 45-55 minutes or until toothpick comes out clean.

mario's cocoa vanilla shake

No time to cook breakfast? Try my ten-year-old's morning shake.

Preparation time: 5 minutes | Cook time: 2 minutes | Yield: 3 (8 oz. glasses)

Ingredients:

4 cups milk
1 teaspoon cocoa powder (chocolate Nesquick works too)
1 cup oats
¼ teaspoon ground cinnamon
1 teaspoon ground vanilla
1/3 cup sugar
½ cup sliced almonds

Blend all ingredients and serve immediately.

corn and coconut vanilla fritters

Preparation time: 15 minutes | Cook time: 20 minutes | Yield: 1 dozen

Ingredients:

1 can creamed corn
1 cup unsweetened coconut
1 cup sugar
1 cup buttermilk (or just milk)
1/3 cup vegetable oil or vanilla oil
1/8 teaspoon baking soda
4 teaspoons baking powder
2 cups all purpose flour
1 tablespoon vanilla extract
1 teaspoon ground vanilla
2 eggs
pinch of salt
vegetable oil for frying

Preparation:

Preheat a frying pan on medium high and pour in the oil. In a large mixing bowl whisk the eggs. Add sugar, vanilla oil, buttermilk, creamed corn, coconut, vanilla extract, and ground vanilla. Put aside.

In another mixing bowl, add all of the dry ingredients and mix them with the coconut-corn mixture. Whisk until all of the ingredients are well blended, but do not over mix.

Drop spoonfuls into the frying oil and remove from heat when both sides are golden brown. Transfer fritters to a platter topped with a paper towel to absorb the oil. Serve warm.

french toast with orange-vanilla butter

Preparation time: 10 minutes | Cook time: 25 minutes | Yield: 12 French toasts

Ingredients:

12 whole wheat sandwich bread slices
2 eggs
1 cup of milk
2 - 3 tablespoons orange-vanilla butter (Recipe follows.)
French vanilla whipped cream or vanilla ice cream
powdered sugar (optional)
fresh fruit for garnish

Preparation:

In a glass Pyrex bowl, whisk eggs and add milk. Stir well until the eggs and milk are thoroughly mixed. Melt the butter, ½ tablespoon at a time, in a large skillet. Once the butter is bubbling, quickly soak the bread slices in the milk mixture. Make sure both sides of the bread are soaked. Put the bread into the skillet and cook until golden brown on both sides.

Serve with a generous dollop of French vanilla whipped cream or vanilla ice cream. Pour fresh fruit on top and sprinkle with powdered sugar.

These are great with the orange-vanilla butter. See Starters, Soups, and Salads section.

superduper granola

Preparation time: 40 minutes | Cook time: 1 hour 30 minutes

Ingredients:

8 cups quick oats
¾ cup brown sugar
½ cup whole wheat flour
1 cup whole wheat fiber
1 cup peanuts
1 cup chopped walnuts
1 cup raisins
1 cup dried apple (or favorite assorted dried fruits)
1 cup unsweetened dried coconut
1 cup unsalted sunflower seeds
3 tablespoons ground vanilla
3 tablespoons ground cinnamon
1 cup peanut oil (or vegetable oil)
1 cup honey
1 cup peanut butter
1 tablespoon vanilla extract

Preparation:

Preheat the oven to 200 degrees. In a small saucepan, warm the oil, honey, peanut butter, and vanilla extract. Stir until all ingredients are fully incorporated. Do not boil. Turn off the stove and put aside.

In a large mixing bowl add oats, brown sugar, whole wheat flour, whole wheat fiber, peanuts, chopped walnuts, raisins, dried apple, coconut, sunflower seeds, ground vanilla, and cinnamon. Stir until the ingredients are mixed well. Pour the peanut butter sauce into dried ingredients little by little, stirring every time until the entire oat mixture is fully coated with the peanut butter mixture.

Spray two 9x11 glass Pyrex dishes with non-stick oil and pour in granola. Cook for approximately 1 hour stirring every 30 minutes (or until granola is completely dried).

breakfast "bagel-cakes"

Yield: 12 servings

Ingredients

12 freshly baked bagels
1 pint heavy cream
3 tablespoons cream cheese (at room temperature)
2 tablespoons granulated sugar
1 vanilla bean, scraped
1 teaspoon vanilla extract
½ teaspoon fresh lemon or orange zest (optional)
fresh fruit

Preparation:

Cream the cheese with the mixer and add the vanilla bean seeds. Add heavy cream and beat at medium high until it starts thickening. Add sugar, vanilla extract, and zest and beat until it forms hard peaks.

Cut the bagels in half and smear on cream cheese mixture. Slice fresh fruit and put on top.

vanilla butternut squash french toast

Preparation time: 50 minutes | Cook time: 35 minutes | Yield: 8+ French toasts

Ingredients:

1 small butternut squash
¾ cups sugar
1 vanilla bean
1½ cups flour
1½ cups milk
½ teaspoon ground cinnamon
pinch of nutmeg
8 slices of sandwich bread
fresh fruit and whipped cream for garnish
vanilla bean syrup

Preparation:

Preheat oven to 400 degrees. Cut butternut squash in half lengthwise, clean from seeds and put on a cookie sheet. Sprinkle it with a little salt and olive or vegetable oil. Put into the oven for 40 minutes. Once cooked, scrape the meat out of the squash and set it apart.

Sift flour, cinnamon, nutmeg, vanilla bean seeds, and sugar in a large bowl. Add milk and squash and stir until the batter has thickened. In a frying pan, melt a little butter and dip the bread slices in the batter and fry until golden brown.

Layer the French toast, put fresh fruit on top, the whipped cream, and then another French toast on top. Pour vanilla syrup on top and enjoy your breakfast!!

vanilla pecan waffles

Preparation time: 15 minutes | Cook time: 30 – 45 minutes | Yield: 15-20 waffles

Ingredients:

1 ½ cups all-purpose flour
½ cup ground pecans
1 cup vanilla sugar
5 teaspoons baking powder
¼ teaspoon salt
3 eggs
1 tablespoon vanilla extract
1 teaspoon ground vanilla
1 ¾ cups milk
2 tablespoons unsalted butter, melted
whipped cream, or vanilla bean syrup

Preparation:

In a mixing bowl combine flour, ground pecans, sugar, baking powder, ground vanilla, and salt. In the second bowl mix together eggs and vanilla extract. Whisk the milk and butter into the egg mixture.

Mix the dry ingredients into the wet ingredients. Stir until combined. Pour batter onto a preheated, lightly greased waffle iron. Bake according to the manufacturer's directions for the waffle iron (about 5-6 minutes) until golden brown and lightly crisp. Serve hot with whipped cream, fresh fruit, or vanilla bean syrup.

Garnish with chopped pecans.

vanilla apple pancakes

Preparation time: 15 minutes | Cook time: 25 minutes | Yield: 20 pancakes

Ingredients:

2 red apples
2 eggs
1 tablespoon vanilla extract
½ cup raisins
½ cup sugar
½ cup chopped walnuts
1 vanilla bean split lengthwise
1/3 cup oil
2 ½ cups milk
2 cups of all purpose flour
6 teaspoons baking powder
A pinch of salt

Preparation:

Shred the apples and put aside. Preheat pancake grill to 350 degrees. Marinate raisins with vanilla extract and put aside. Whisk the egg in a large bowl and add sugar, oil, vanilla bean seeds, shredded apples, walnuts, and raisins.

Sift flour, baking soda, and salt in a smaller bowl and add this mixture to the egg mixture alternating with milk. Whisk all of the ingredients until they are thoroughly blended, but do not over whisk. Spray grill with a non-stick cooking oil and pour dough with a big spoon. Let it cook until you see bubbles on the pancake's surface (about two minutes). Turn your pancakes and remove from heat when they are golden brown in both sides.

Serve hot with a whipped cream topping or vanilla syrup.

Note: You can substitute vanilla bean by using both vanilla sugar and vanilla oil. You can also add 1 teaspoon of ground cinnamon to your batter.

banana vanilla fritters

Preparation time: 15 minutes | Cook time: 20 minutes | Yield: 15 fritters

Ingredients:

2 ripe bananas
1 cup buttermilk (or just milk)
1/3 cup vegetable oil or vanilla oil
1/8 teaspoon baking soda
4 teaspoons baking powder
1 ¼ cup all purpose flour
1 tablespoon vanilla extract
2 eggs
pinch of salt
vanilla powdered sugar
cocoa powder
ground cinnamon
vegetable oil for frying

Preparation:

Preheat a frying pan on medium high and pour in the oil. Peel and smash the ripe the bananas in a small bowl and put them aside. Whisk the eggs in a large bowl and add the vanilla extract and vegetable oil. In another bowl sift the flour, baking soda, baking powder, salt, and sugar. Add the dry ingredients to the egg mixture and whisk until all of the ingredients are well mixed, but do not over mix.

Spoon the batter into the frying pan with a spoon and deep fry until both sides are dark golden brown. Remove from heat and season with ground cinnamon. Before serving, sprinkle fritters with vanilla powdered sugar and cocoa powder. Serve warm.

6 : starters :
spreads, soups, salads dressings, & side dishes

Vanilla is a natural enhancer for any type of vegetable dish. Since most fruits and veggies produce limited amounts of natural vanillin, adding vanilla to the dish will bring out the natural sweetness and flavor of almost any type of vegetable. Additionally, vanilla oils and vanilla vinegars make great salad dressings. Using vanilla oil in vinaigrette, especially fruit vinaigrettes, really brings out the natural sweetness and enhances the fruitiness in the dressings and salads.

A great way to start is by using vanilla infused oils. You saw a simple vanilla oil recipe in the first Basics section, but this section includes several ideas on herbal and vanilla oils to show the versatility of vanilla oils and vinegars. Your imagination really is the limit! Let those creative vanilla juices flow and your salads will have never been so happy!

6.1 : salads and salads dressings :

vanilla herbed oil

Yield: 1 ¾ cup

Ingredients:

2 vanilla beans
1 garlic clove
1 sprig rosemary
1 sprig thyme
2 sage leaves
1 ½ cup vegetable oil

Preparation:

Heat oil in a saucepan. Cut the vanilla beans lengthwise and scrape the seeds. Add the pods and seeds to the oil at low/medium heat. Do not burn the seeds. Whisk them until they are blended with the oil and remove from heat. Take the vanilla pods out and save them for later.

Chop the garlic clove, sage leaves, and thyme. Put them aside.

Pour oil into a measuring cup. Put the garlic, sage, and thyme into a bottle and pour the vanilla oil on top. Take the vanilla pods and the rosemary spring and put them inside the bottle and seal it. Let it sit in your pantry for at least 8 days before using. This oil is perfect for sautéed mushrooms, pan fried fish, pork, or chicken. It can also be used for salad dressings, marinades, and vinaigrettes.

spinach and strawberry salad

Preparation time: 25 minutes | Yield: 5 servings

Ingredients:

1 lb. baby spinach
2 cups sliced strawberries
1 cup chopped walnuts
orange vanilla vinaigrette

Preparation:

Put the baby spinach in a large salad bowl. Add the sliced strawberries and the orange vinaigrette. Gently toss them and sprinkle the chopped walnuts. Add orange vanilla vinaigrette. Toss lightly.

lemongrass, cilantro, and vanilla vinegar

Ingredients:

1 large stalk fresh lemongrass, top and end removed
2 vanilla beans
¼ cup fresh cilantro
pinch of salt
4 cups rice wine vinegar

Preparation:

Roughly chop the lemongrass and cilantro. Add to the vinegar in a blender. Split and scrape the vanilla beans adding both the beans and the scraped pod to the vinegar. Add a pinch of salt.

Blend all ingredients until almost completely liquefied.

Place liquid in an airtight container and allow to sit undisturbed for one week. Strain the liquid out through a coffee filter (Note: Do not shake the contents up before straining. This leads to a cloudy finished vinegar and does not produce any different results.) Store in a dark glass or plastic container.

For more flavor and a great look store the vinegar in a clear glass container adding a split vanilla bean, sprig of cilantro, and long pieces of lemongrass.

lobster vanilla salad in butter lettuce bowl

Yield: 4 servings

Ingredients:

2 fresh or frozen lobster tails
1 pound of butter, cut into cubes
¼ cup of water
2 Tahitian vanilla beans, split and scraped reserving both the empty pod and the beans
kosher salt
½ cup celeriac, finely chopped
½ cup red bell pepper, finely chopped
¼ cup carrot, finely chopped
2 shallots, finely chopped
1 tablespoon fresh thyme, chopped
1 tablespoon fresh parsley, chopped
1 tablespoon fresh tarragon, chopped
1 tablespoon fresh mint, chopped
1 cup of crème fraiche
 kosher salt
ground black pepper
2 heads of butter lettuce

Preparation:

In a medium sauce pot bring the water up to almost a boiling point. Remove from heat and whisk in the cubed butter. If the butter stops melting, return to the heat briefly and then remove and continue whisking until all of the butter is dissolved. Do not overheat and break the emulsion of the butter! Add the vanilla beans and scraped pods. Season with salt until you get a rich buttery taste.

Chop the lobster tails into ½ inch cubes. Slowly poach the lobster meat in the vanilla butter over low heat until it is cooked through. Remove from the butter and chill.
In a large bowl combine the cooked and chilled lobster meat, celeriac, red bell pepper, carrot, thyme, parsley, tarragon, mint, and crème fraiche. Mix well to combine and thoroughly coat the meat. Adjust seasoning with salt and ground black pepper.

On each plate stack individual leaves of lettuce together to form a bowl. Spoon ¼ of the salad mix into the center of the lettuce bowl.

orange vanilla vinaigrette

Preparation time: 5 minutes | Yield: 1 cup

Ingredients:

½ cup white vinegar
½ cup orange juice
1 tablespoon vanilla sugar
1 teaspoon vanilla extract
½ teaspoon orange zest

Preparation:

Combine white vinegar, orange juice, vanilla sugar, vanilla extract, and orange zest into a bowl. Whisk together until all of the ingredients are thoroughly mixed.

This vinaigrette should be used the same day; otherwise the orange zest will make it turn bitter.

apple cider vinaigrette

Preparation time: 5 minutes | Yield: 1 bottle

Ingredients:

1 bottle apple cider vinegar
4 vanilla beans cut lengthwise

Preparation:

Scrape the vanilla beans and put the seeds into the vinegar. Shake well until the seeds have incorporated in the vinegar. Add the pods. Seal and keep it in a cool dark place. (Your kitchen cupboard would be a great place.)

vanilla, cilantro, ginger, and serrano pepper infused white wine vinegar

Preparation time: 45-50 minutes | Chilled time: 1 week | Yield: Approximately 3 cups

Ingredients:

2 whole Madagascar vanilla beans
½ bunch fresh cilantro
1, 2-inch long fresh ginger root
2 whole serrano peppers
4 cups white wine vinegar
pinch of salt

Preparation:

Cut vanilla beans lengthwise and scrape out beans. Add vanilla pods and scraped beans to vinegar. Roughly chop the ginger and cilantro. Add both to the vinegar. Remove the top of the peppers and cut them in half lengthwise. If you want to have less pepper heat in the vinegar, remove the seeds and discard. Add the peppers to the vinegar.

Place all the ingredients into a blender and add the pinch of salt. Puree ingredients until they are almost completely liquefied. Place liquid in an airtight container and allow to sit undisturbed for one week.

Strain the liquid out through a coffee filter. (Note: Do not shake the contents up before straining. This leads to a cloudy finished vinegar and does not produce any different results.) Store in a dark glass or plastic container.

For more flavor and a great look store the vinegar in a clear glass container adding a split vanilla bean, cilantro, piece of ginger, and half a serrano pepper.

coriander vanilla sauce

Makes 1 Pint

Ingredients:

½ cup onions, sliced no larger than ¼ inch thick
¼ cup celery, sliced no larger than ¼ inch thick
3 tablespoons coriander seeds
1 large Madagascar vanilla bean
1 bay leaf
6 fresh thyme sprigs
2 teaspoons of butter
1 teaspoon minced fresh garlic
vegetable stock (broth) as needed
kosher salt

Optional:
fish stock (as needed) with 1 cup fresh oyster juice
chicken stock, as needed

Preparation:

Melt the butter over low heat in a large sauce pan and add the onions, celery, and garlic. Split and scrape the vanilla bean and add both the scraped inside beans and the empty pod to the onions and celery along with the thyme sprigs and bay leaf. Season lightly with salt. Cover the pan and allow the ingredients to start sweating (turning limp).

In a small dry pan, toast the coriander seeds over high heat until they become fragrant and start to smoke slightly. Combine with other ingredients and finish sweating the mixture (covered) until the vegetables are translucent. Do not allow them to take on any color.

Add enough vegetable stock to cover all of the ingredients by ½ to 1 inch. Increase the heat to a simmer and allow the sauce to simmer and reduce to ½ to ¾ of the original volume. Do not allow the sauce to boil.

Once sauce is reduced, carefully strain through a fine mesh strainer (chinois) or damp cheesecloth discarding the ingredients. Season the sauce to taste with salt. If you desire a little more richness or if the sauce is over-salted, whisk in butter 1 tablespoon at a time over low heat.

Optional: Depending on what you want to serve this with, you may change the liquid used to match that protein. For example, if this sauce is going on a cilantro braised pork chop, then make the sauce with chicken stock.

vanilla, rosemary, and white balsamic vinegar

Preparation: 25 – 35 minutes | Chilled time: 1 week | Yield: 1 ½ cups

Ingredients:

2 bourbon vanilla beans
1 fresh rosemary sprig
2 cups white balsamic vinegar

Preparation:

Cut and scrape vanilla pods. Add the pods and the scraped beans to the vinegar.
Strip all the leaves off the rosemary and add to the vinegar.

Combine all of the ingredients and puree in a blender until all contents are liquefied.
Place liquid in an airtight container and allow to sit undisturbed for one week.

Strain liquid through a coffee filter. (Note: Do not shake liquid before straining. This
leads to a cloudy final liquid and does not produce any better flavor.) Place strained
liquid in a dark glass or plastic container. For more flavors, add a sprig of rosemary and
one split vanilla bean to the vinegar.

carrot raisin salad

Yield: 4 servings

Ingredients:

1 lb. shredded carrots
1 cup raisins
1 tablespoon sugar
1 teaspoon vanilla extract
¾ Miracle Whip (or mayonnaise)

Preparation :

Mix the Miracle Whip with vanilla extract and sugar. Stir until all ingredients are blended. Put aside.
In a medium salad bowl, mix carrots with raisins. Add the Miracle Whip dressing and toss to coat.

orange infused vanilla champagne vinegar

Ingredients:

zest of one large orange, all pith (white stuff) removed
4 vanilla beans
4 cups champagne vinegar
pinch of salt

Preparation:

Split vanilla pods lengthwise and scrape all the beans from the inside. Add both the beans and the scraped pods to the vinegar in a blender.

Add cleaned orange zest to the vinegar. Add a pinch of salt and puree ingredients until they are all almost liquid.

Place liquid in an airtight container and allow to sit undisturbed for one week. Strain the liquid out through a coffee filter. (Note: Do not shake the contents up before straining. This leads to a cloudy finished vinegar and does not produce any different results.) Store in a dark glass or plastic container.

For more flavor and a great look store the vinegar in a clear glass container adding a split vanilla bean and several long strips of orange peel.

vanilla roasted fennel salad

Yield: 4-6 servings

Ingredients:

Vanilla Roasted Fennel:

2 vanilla beans
2 whole fennel bulbs
½ cup olive oil
kosher salt
ground black pepper

Salad:

1 cup grape tomatoes
¼ cup sliced almonds
1 Anjou pear
1 cup three-year-old Gouda cheese

Vinaigrette:

½ cup cilantro, ginger, serrano pepper, and vanilla vinegar
½ cup olive oil
1 tablespoon fresh thyme, finely chopped
1 tablespoon of fresh parsley, finely chopped
kosher salt
ground black pepper
dash of Tabasco

Preparation:

Cut the stalks and fronds off of the bulbs of fennel. Cut the bulbs of fennel into quarters and remove the center stalk.

Toss the quartered bulbs of fennel and the scraped vanilla beans into the olive oil (use both the beans scraped from the pods and the empty pods for the roasting process).

6.2 : spreads :

Another great way to use vanilla is in spreads for breads, muffins, and even bagels. I would like to share a couple of my favorite spreads using vanilla – actually any time!

easy sweet orange-vanilla butter

Preparation time: 10 minutes | Yield: 2 cups

Ingredients:

2 cups unsalted butter, softened
2 tablespoons vanilla sugar
¼ teaspoons vanilla paste (ground vanilla or 1 vanilla bean)
1/8 teaspoon dried orange zest

Preparation:

Mix all ingredients. Store it in an airtight container in the refrigerator.

peanut butter and vanilla spread

Preparation time: 4 minutes

Ingredients:

1 cup peanut butter (smooth or crunchy), softened
1 tablespoon honey
1/4 teaspoon vanilla paste (ground vanilla or 1 vanilla bean)

Preparation:

Mix all of the ingredients until thoroughly incorporated. Fresh fruit would go with it for a more nutritional breakfast.

tomato balsamic jam

Makes 1 quart

Ingredients:

15 Roma tomatoes (or 5 regular tomatoes) bottoms removed, quartered, and cut into ½ inch pieces
5 ounces balsamic vinegar
2 ½ cups sugar
¼ bunch fresh thyme (about 20 sprigs)
1 vanilla beans, cut and scraped reserving only the beans
1 teaspoon kosher salt
½ large yellow onion, chopped into ½ inch pieces
2 tablespoons olive oil
½ teaspoon red pepper flakes
½ teaspoon whole allspice
½ teaspoon whole celery seed
½ whole star anise
1 dried bay leaf
2 whole cloves
9 ounces tomato juice

Preparation:

Warm the onions over low heat in the olive oil until they are translucent in a large saucepan. Add sugar, salt, balsamic vinegar, tomatoes, and tomato juice to the onions and bring to a simmer.

Combine the red pepper flakes, allspice, celery seed, star anise, bay leaves, and cloves in a spice grinder (a coffee grinder or commercial blender work well also) and grind until all the ingredients are powdered with no large pieces. Add to the simmering jam and stir to mix well.

Strip the leaves of the fresh thyme from the stalks discarding the stalks. Roughly chop up the leaves and add them to the jam, again stirring well to completely combine. Allow the jam to reduce to simmer until it has reached a string consistency. (Test by placing a small amount of jam on your thumb and smash together using your forefinger. Gently separate your fingers about ¼ inch apart. If the jam forms a string that does not break then the jam is ready.)

Keep the jam in an airtight container in the refrigerator.

vanilla cream cheese spread

Preparation time: 5 minutes | Yield: 1 ½ cups

Ingredients:

8 oz cream cheese, softened
2 tablespoons honey
1/4 teaspoon vanilla paste (ground vanilla or 1 vanilla bean)
1 tablespoon raisins
1 tablespoon chopped walnuts

Preparation:

Mix all of the ingredients thoroughly in the food processor until they are well blended.

6.3 : sides :

vanilla herbed mushrooms

Preparation: 5 minutes | Cook time: 20 minutes | Yield: 5-6 servings

Ingredients:

2 12-oz. packages of mushrooms
1 spring fresh parsley
1 spring fresh thyme
5 leaves fresh sage
2 leaves fresh basil
½ spring fresh rosemary
1 Tahitian vanilla bean, split and scraped
2 chopped garlic gloves
½ cup vegetable oil
salt and pepper to taste

Preparation:

Heat oil in a large skillet at medium to high heat. Split the vanilla bean, scrape the seeds inside, and put both into the skillet. Let it cook for approximately two minutes until the seeds have incorporated into the oil. Add the mushrooms and sauté for five minutes. Add fresh chopped herbs, garlic, salt, and pepper. Sauté for fifteen more minutes until mushrooms look golden brown. Remove vanilla bean and serve.

Note: We choose the Tahitian vanilla bean for this recipe because its earthly aroma compliments the mushrooms. This recipe has not been tested with other kinds of vanilla beans or extract.

vanilla baby carrots and raisins

Preparation time: 2 minutes | Cook time: 10 minutes | Yield: 5-6 servings

Ingredients

1 pound baby carrots
1 tablespoon butter
1 teaspoon vanilla extract
1 teaspoon brown sugar
½ cup raisins

Preparation:

Mix raisins with vanilla extract in a small bowl and put aside. Melt butter at medium heat in a medium-sized sauté pan. Add baby carrots and sugar. Stir. Add the raisins and vanilla extract. Cook on medium to high heat for 5 to 7 minutes. Remove from heat and serve warm. The baby carrots should still be crunchy.

green beans with orange-vanilla butter

Preparation time: 5 minutes | Cook time: 20 minutes | Yield: 6-7 servings

Ingredients:

2 lbs. frozen green beans
4 tablespoons orange-vanilla butter (recipe below)
1 cup slivered almonds
salt to taste

Orange-Vanilla Butter

1 cup butter (room temperature)
½ teaspoon vanilla paste
pinch of dried orange zest

Preparation:

In a large skillet melt the butter and add the frozen green beans. Add salt to taste and sauté for about 20 minutes at medium-high heat. Garnish with slivered almonds and serve immediately.

yellow curry

Makes 1 ½ Quarts

Ingredients:

1 lb. banana peppers, tops and stems removed
10 cloves fresh garlic
3 inch peeled fresh ginger root
½ bunch fresh cilantro (1oz.)
2 tablespoons coriander seed, toasted and ground
1 vanilla bean, split and scraped reserving only the inside beans
zest of 2 lemons
zest and juice of 4 limes
2 teaspoons turmeric
2 tablespoons mustard powder
1 cup of mustard oil
kosher salt

Preparation:

Roughly chop the ginger and banana peppers into pieces no larger than ½ inch. Combine all ingredients into a food processor and process until all the ingredients are well chopped and of uniform size.

Adjust seasoning if necessary. Place the curry in glass containers half full and allow to rest in the sun for 3 to 5 days.

When curry comes out of the sun, process in a blender until smooth.

habeñero green curry

Makes 1 ½ Quarts

Ingredients:

1 pound habañero peppers, tops and seeds removed. (Note: Wear gloves when dealing with these peppers! Do not touch your face or any other parts of your body while cutting them. Wash all equipment and hands thoroughly before proceeding.)
6 stalks fresh lemongrass (base, top, and outer layers removed)
1 tablespoon fresh thyme
2 tablespoons green peppercorns
4 tablespoons capers
zest of 2 oranges
1 bunch fresh mint (3/4 oz.)
1 bunch fresh cilantro (2 oz.)
8 oz. peeled fresh ginger root
¼ cup fresh garlic
2 Madagascar vanilla beans, split and scraped retaining only the inside beans
6 Kafir lime leaves (use the zest of 4 limes to substitute)
1½ tablespoon turmeric
1 tablespoon mustard powder
1 tablespoon celery seed
1 teaspoon whole allspice
6 whole cloves
3 tablespoons coriander
3 bay leaves
1½ cups mustard oil, to bind
kosher salt

Preparation:

In a small sauté pan combine the celery seed, allspice, coriander, and cloves. Toast them over high heat until they just start to smoke. Immediately remove them from the heat and from the pan. Grind all the toasted spices along with the bay leaves in a spice grinder.

Roughly chop the lemongrass and ginger root into pieces no larger than ½ inch. Combine all of the ingredients including the toasted and ground spices in a food processor. Season with 1 tablespoon of salt and process until all the ingredients have been well chopped and are of similar size.

Remove from the food processor and place in glass jars only halfway full. Allow the curry to sit in the sun for 3 to 5 days. When curry is done process in a blender until you have a smooth consistency.

Caution: This curry is extremely hot.

brochettes with sun-dried tomato pesto sauce

Preparation time: 25 minutes | Cook time: 20 minutes | Yield: 5 servings

Ingredients:

20 slices diagonally sliced wheat bread (or French bread)
20 thin slices mozzarella
1 tablespoon dried oregano
sun-dried tomato pesto (recipe follows)

Sun Dried Tomato Pesto

Ingredients:

2 small packages of sun-dried tomatoes (re-hydrated)
1 small chopped onion
2 chopped garlic cloves
1 chopped green bell pepper
½ cup chopped fresh parsley
1 cup vanilla oil
salt and pepper

Preparation:

Put all of the pesto ingredients (except for the oil) in the food processor. Blend with the Pause button a couple of times. Add salt and pepper, and then press the Low button. Start adding the vanilla oil very carefully to emulsify it. Turn off and set aside.

Preheat the oven to 400 degrees. Toast the bread for ten minutes. Remove from heat and turn the bread slices with the toasted side up. Place the mozzarella on the bread slices, and then spoon the pesto on top of the cheese. Sprinkle with dried oregano. Set the oven on broil and cook brochettes for 30 seconds to one minute until the cheese is melted.

Remove from heat and move to a separate dish. Serve immediately.

sweet potato fries

Preparation time: 20 minutes | Cook time: 20 minutes | Yield: 4 servings

Ingredients:

4 sweet potatoes
1 tablespoon vanilla sugar (or granulated sugar and 1 vanilla bean scraped)
¼ teaspoon ground cinnamon
2 cups peanut oil (any vegetable oil would work fine)

Preparation:

Preheat fryer to 375 degrees. Peel the sweet potatoes and slice them very thickly. Mix vanilla sugar and cinnamon and put them into a small container. Set aside. Once oil is hot, carefully put in the potato slices and cook for approximately five minutes or until thoroughly cooked. Quickly remove from frying pan and put on a plate. Season the fries with vanilla sugar and cinnamon mixture while they are still hot. Serve immediately.

cauliflower casserole with vanilla squash sauce

Preparation time: 35 minutes | Cook time: 20 minutes | Yield: 7-9 servings

Ingredients:

1 head cauliflower
2 tablespoons butter
2 cans chicken broth (13.75 oz. cans)
1 chopped large clove garlic
1 chopped medium onion
1 teaspoon vanilla extract
4 tablespoons cornstarch (or flour)
pinch of nutmeg
1 package frozen squash
3 tablespoons buttermilk (substitute milk or half-and-half)
salt and pepper

Preparation:

Preheat oven to 400 degrees. Cut up the cauliflower florets and put aside. Melt butter and sauté the onion with the garlic. Add the cornstarch and stir. Add the chicken broth and whisk until all the ingredients are blended. Add the squash (frozen), nutmeg, buttermilk, and vanilla extract. Remove from heat and season with salt and pepper, and then blend with a hand blender.

Season the cauliflower florets with salt and pepper then put into large buttered Pyrex and pour sauce on top. Put into the oven for 20 minutes. Remove from oven and serve warm. The cauliflower should be cooked but still crunchy.

spiced vanilla zucchini bread

Makes 2 two-pound loaves

Ingredients:

3 cups whole wheat flour
2 teaspoons of ground cinnamon
1 teaspoon ground allspice
½ teaspoon ground nutmeg
1 teaspoon baking soda
1 teaspoon kosher salt
¾ teaspoon baking powder
1 tablespoon lemon zest
1 tablespoon orange zest
2 Madagascar vanilla beans, split and scraped
2 cups grated fresh zucchini (save any juice)
1 cup walnuts, toasted and roughly chopped
2 cups vanilla sugar (white granulated)
1 cup vegetable oil
4 large white eggs

Preparation:

Combine all dry ingredients except for the sugar (flour, cinnamon, allspice, nutmeg, baking soda, baking powder, salt) and sift together into a large bowl. In another bowl combine the eggs and sugar and whisk together until the eggs become a pale yellow color and all the sugar is dissolved.

Add the zests of the lemons and oranges to the sugar and eggs and whisk well to combine. Add the oil and whisk until all the oil is blended. Finally add the scraped vanilla beans. Whisk well to combine.

Fold the sifted dry ingredients into the egg mixture a quarter at a time. Once all the dry ingredients are incorporated, add the grated zucchini and any juice from the zucchini. Fold in completely.

Grease 2 two-pound loaf pans and divide the batter evenly into the pans. Bake at 350 degrees for about 1 hour.

honduran coconut rolls

Preparation time: 20 minutes | Inactive time: 3-4 hours | Yield: 2 dozen

Ingredients:

2 cups all-purpose flour
1 tablespoon yeast
1/8 teaspoon salt
½ cup sugar
1 large egg, slightly beaten
1 cup coconut milk
2 tablespoons soft margarine, melted
1 teaspoon vanilla extract

Preparation:

Sift dry ingredients into a bowl. Combine sugar, beaten egg, coconut milk, melted margarine, and vanilla in another bowl. Add dry ingredients to the milk mixture and knead until all ingredients are thoroughly incorporated. Do not over knead. Five minutes should be enough.

Shape the dough into a ball and cover. Let it rise. When it has doubled in size (approximately 2 hours) pinch the dough and form into little rolls. Let it rise again (1 hour).

Preheat the oven to 375 degrees and place the rolls on a greased cookie sheet. Cover and let it rise again. Once the dough has risen, (about 1 more hour) bake the rolls for approximately 30 minutes or until done.

baked vanilla plantains

Preparation: 10 minutes | Cook time: 20 minutes | Yield: 5 servings

Ingredients:

6 ripe plantains (yellow with black stripes)
1 teaspoon vanilla sugar (or regular sugar and 1 scraped vanilla bean)
¼ teaspoon ground cinnamon

Preparation:

Preheat the oven to 400 degrees. Mix the vanilla sugar and ground cinnamon. Put aside. Spray a cookie sheet with non-stick cooking oil. Cut the ends of the plantains, peel, and cut them diagonally into ½ inch (approx.) strips. Place them on the cookie sheet and spray with oil.

Bake for 20 minutes. Remove from heat and season with the vanilla sugar and cinnamon mix and put back into the oven for 10 more minutes.
Take them out of the oven and serve warm.

spiced tortilla crisp

Ingredients:

1 packet six-inch corn tortillas cut into quarters
½ cup granulated sugar (vanilla sugar is recommended)
2 tablespoons kosher salt (or sea salt)
1 tablespoon pure ground vanilla
½ teaspoon mustard powder
½ teaspoon cayenne pepper
1 pinch cinnamon
1 pinch nutmeg
1 pinch allspice

Preparation:

Combine all ingredients in a bowl (except for the tortillas).
Deep fry the chips until crisp.
Remove from the oil and drain well.
Liberally sprinkle the seasoning over the chips.

These chips go very well with Avocado Ice Cream.

tomato salad with white balsamic vinaigrette

Preparation time: 20 minutes | Yield: 2-3 servings

Ingredients:

12 Roma tomatoes, sliced
salt to taste

White Balsamic Vinaigrette

1 teaspoon fresh rosemary
4 leafs fresh mint
2 tablespoons white balsamic vinaigrette
2 tablespoons vanilla oil
A pinch of coriander
1/8 teaspoon ground cumin
Salt

Preparation:

Mix all of the ingredients for the vinaigrette in a bowl. Pour over sliced tomatoes and stir. Re-season before serving if needed.

thai marinated olives

Ingredients:

1 cup rice wine vinegar
¼ cup honey (tangerine or orange honey works best)
¼ cup sesame oil
¼ cup ginger, roughly chopped
3 fresh garlic cloves cut in half with the green germ removed
6 scallions (green spring onions), cut into two-inch sections
2 red chili peppers cut in half with seeds removed
2 tablespoons sweet soy sauce
1 bourbon vanilla bean
4 cups pitted green queen olives
1 cup grapeseed oil
¼ cup fresh cilantro (best to keep the leaves on the stalk for easier removal later)
zest of 2 limes
kosher salt
ground black pepper

Preparation:

In a large sauté pan over low heat warm the ginger, garlic, scallions, and peppers in sesame oil until peppers start to soften (sweat), about 5 to 10 minutes. Add scraped vanilla pods and cook for 2 to 3 more minutes.

Add honey, grapeseed oil, sweet soy sauce, lime zest, vanilla beans (scraped from the pods), and cilantro to the mixture and remove from heat.

Season to taste with salt and pepper. Remember that the olives will retain a good amount of their natural salinity. If the marinade seems just a bit under seasoned this will be fine as the salt in the olives will bring the seasoning up to the right level.

As the mixture starts to cool add the olives and mix well to coat the olives entirely.

Store olives in a glass jar or large plastic container. Store in a cool dark place (they do not need to be refrigerated) for a week before eating. Stir the olives once a day.
Note: Olives can be eaten immediately and will have good flavor. Allowing them to marinate for a week before eating allows all the flavors to penetrate the thick interior of the olives. The olives should be eaten within a month of marinating.

6.4 : soups :

mexican squash (chayote) and pear soup

Preparation time: 35 minutes | Cook time: 25 minutes | Yield: 6 servings

Ingredients:

3 medium Mexican squash (chayote)
2 soft skinned pears
½ chopped onion
1 cup half-and-half
½ cup water
1 teaspoon vanilla extract
1 tablespoon butter
 pinch of ground nutmeg
salt
pepper

Preparation:

Cut off the tops and bottoms of the squash. Cut the squash in half and remove the heart. Cut lengthwise and dice. Put into a medium sized bowl of warm water. Cut the pears in half and core them. Slice lengthwise and dice.

Meanwhile, melt the butter in a deep pan and sauté the chopped onion, about 2 minutes. Add the squash and the pears. Sauté until their volume is reduced in half. The fruits should be very soft. Add the half-and-half, vanilla extract, water, nutmeg, salt and pepper to taste. Stir well and let cool.

Once it is cool, put the mixture in a food processor or a blender and blend it until it has a coarse consistency
Serve warm or cold.

vanilla coconut seafood soup

Preparation time: 45 minutes | Cook time: 30 minutes | Yield: 12 servings

Ingredients:

1 pound halibut (or any white fish)
1 pound cod
1 pound peeled and de-veined shrimp
½ pound diced scallops
1 Mexican squash
3 tablespoons butter
1 tablespoon chopped fresh ginger
2 ½ cups chopped baby carrots
3 chopped celery ribs
2 chopped garlic cloves
2 cans water chestnuts (8oz.each)
1 cup chopped green onions
1 diced large onion
1 teaspoon vanilla extract
¼ teaspoon dried thyme
3 tablespoons chicken bouillon
1/8 teaspoon garlic powder
¼ teaspoon onion powder
4 tablespoons flour
½ ounce ground shrimp
2 cans coconut milk (13.5 oz. each)
½ cup milk
1 cup water
4 cans chicken broth (14 oz. cans)
salt and pepper to taste
paprika and chopped chives for garnish

Preparation:

In a large, deep soup pan (or Dutch oven) melt the butter and sauté the onions, carrots, celery, ginger, chopped garlic and Mexican squash. After approximately ten minutes, add the flour and stir for about 30 seconds. Add the chicken broth, the coconut milk, ground shrimp, chicken bouillon, onion powder, garlic powder, vanilla, and water. Stir and let simmer for 10-15 minutes. Stir constantly to prevent milk from sticking to the bottom of the pan.

Meanwhile, cut the fish and scallops in small pieces and season with salt, pepper, and thyme. Finely chop the green onions and put aside.

When the vegetables are fork tender, add the milk, seafood, and green onions. Let simmer for five to seven minutes, stirring constantly. Make sure that the seafood is completely cooked, but do not overcook. Overcooking seafood makes it very difficult to eat.

Serve immediately over white rice. Garnish with sweet paprika and finely chopped chives.

vanilla smoked cauliflower soup with apple spiced mascarpone cheese

Yield: 4-6 servings

Ingredients:

Soup:
1 head cauliflower
1 quart of half-and-half
½ oz. fresh thyme
1 bay leaf (dried or fresh)
½ teaspoon whole black peppercorns
1 tablespoon fresh oregano
1 stalk fresh tarragon
1 Madagascar vanilla pod, scraped and reserving the beans and the outer pod
2 dried empty vanilla pods (pods that have been previously scraped cleaned of beans inside and then dehydrated)
½ pound maple wood chips (or preferred wood chip) presoaked overnight
kosher salt
ground black pepper

Garnish:

½ cup mascarpone cheese
2 tablespoons apple cider vinegar
2 tablespoons granulated sugar
small pinch ground allspice
small pinch kosher salt
4-6 sprigs fresh chervil

Preparation:

Slice the cauliflower head into quarters and remove the inner stalk and all green elements (leaves and stalk). Slice each quarter into ½ inch thick slices. (Do not worry if some of the pieces break off. This is preparing the cauliflower for smoking by exposing the greatest amount of surface area so more of the smoke flavor will be absorbed.) Place the wood chips in a smoker and set the temperature on low. If you do not have a smoker or access to one please use the following directions:

You will need a deep pot that has an insert used for pasta or vegetables that has holes for draining the water and a lid. Line the bottom of the pot with aluminum foil. Tthis will prevent the pot from burning the chips and not ruin the base for further cooking. Drain the wood chips and place them into the pot on top of the aluminum foil. Place the dried vanilla pods on top of the wood chips. Set the pot over high heat until the chips start to smoke slightly. (Note: Watch this very carefully as the wood chips can and will burn.) Reduce the heat to low and cover the pot.

Place all of the sliced cauliflower into the smoker (or into the insert and then place the insert into the pot with the smoking wood chips and cover). Allow the cauliflower to smoke for 2 to 3 hours. Check the amount of smoke being produced by the chips every 30 minutes.

While the cauliflower is smoking, prepare the garnish by combining the mascarpone cheese, apple cider vinegar, salt, and sugar in a mixer with the whisk attachment. Blend on medium high until all the ingredients are thoroughly combined and the sugar and salt are completely dissolved.

Combine the half-and-half, thyme, bay leaf, peppercorns, oregano, tarragon, vanilla beans, and scraped pod in a medium pot. Bring to a simmer and allow the half-and-half to infuse for 20 to 30 minutes. Strain when finished reserving the liquid and discarding everything else. Return the liquid back to the pot. Remove the cauliflower from the smoker and turn off the heat. (Allow the wood chips to cool and remove them from the smoker.) Combine the cauliflower with the half-and-half in the pot and allow to cool slightly.

Once the liquid and cauliflower are no longer hot place in a blender and puree until all the ingredients are smooth and there are no solid pieces. Return the soup to the pot and reheat. Season to taste with salt and ground black pepper.

Ladle the soup into a bowl and place a small spoonful of the apple mascarpone cheese in the center. Garnish the soup with a sprig of fresh chervil on top of the cheese.

celeriac vanilla soup

Makes 2 quarts

Ingredients:

2 large celeriac bulbs, peeled and cut into one-inch cubes
24 sprigs fresh thyme
1 bay leaf
1 teaspoon black peppercorns
½ cup chopped onion
¼ cup chopped leeks
¼ cup chopped celery
4 tablespoons butter
1 Madagascar vanilla bean, split and scraped reserving both the empty pod and beans
1 quart half-and-half
1 quart vegetable stock or broth
kosher salt
ground black pepper

Preparation:

Sweat (cook until soft on low) the onions, leeks, and celery in the butter until soft. Add thyme, bay leaf, peppercorns, and vanilla beans (both). Cook the vegetables with the herbs and spices for 3 to 5 more minutes.

Add the celery, vegetable stock, and half-and-half. Cook at a strong simmer until the celery pieces are fork tender. Allow the soup to cool slightly then process all of the ingredients in a blender until there are no visible chunks. Strain the soup through a fine strainer or cheesecloth. Reheat to serve.

vanilla oyster soup

Preparation time: 35 minutes | Cook time: 20 minutes | Yield: 4 servings

Ingredients:

1 carrot, peeled, halved, and sliced into 1/8 inch pieces
1 large yellow onion, peeled and chopped
2 stalks celery, washed and chopped
4 tablespoon butter
24 large fresh oysters
1 quart half-and-half
1 bay leaf
12 sprigs fresh thyme
1 tablespoon whole black peppercorns
2 teaspoon whole coriander seeds
1 teaspoon fennel seeds
2 Madagascar vanilla beans, cut lengthwise and scraped
2 dashes Tabasco
kosher salt to taste
herbed croutons to garnish

Preparation:

Sweat (cook over low heat) the carrots, onions, and celery in butter and 1 tsp. of salt until all are almost translucent. Add the vanilla beans (the inside of the beans) and cook for one minute.

Add the half-and-half and the oysters. Season with salt to taste. Combine the bay leaf, fresh thyme, peppercorns, coriander, fennel seeds, and the scraped vanilla pods to the soup. Bring soup up to just under a boil then reduce the heat to a simmer. Allow soup to simmer for 15 to 20 minutes.

Remove the vanilla pods and the bay leaf from the soup and discard. Liquefy remaining ingredients (in small batches) in a blender. Strain blended soup through a fine mesh sieve. Add Tabasco and finish by seasoning with salt and pepper to taste. Garnish with herb croutons and serve.

7 : the main course :

Many people, chefs included, don't think about the vanilla in savory dishes. If you ask most individuals, they might think about vanilla only for desserts or maybe breakfasts. Vanilla is good with just about any type of savory dish. Fish, fowl, pork, beef, pastas, sauces – all can be kicked up with vanilla. While you might not taste the vanilla in the dishes, vanilla enhances the natural flavors of just about any dish. The recipes included here are to give you an idea of ways to use the vanilla in savory dishes. The idea is that vanilla will enhance the natural sweetness and flavors of most meats and vegetables. Don't be afraid to experiment with the dishes, especially as to the amount or type of vanilla used, to make them fit your palate.

When a vanilla bean is used in tomato or chile sauces, it can cut the heat and acid by about half. This is a way to use vanilla in traditional Italian and Mexican cuisine.

vanilla red curry

Makes 3 cups

Ingredients:

1 pound small red peppers
8 cloves fresh garlic
1 tablespoon kosher salt
½ cup to 1 cup mustard oil
2 tablespoons mustard powder
2 tablespoons paprika
2 Tahitian vanilla beans, split and scraped retaining the scraped inside beans
4 limes, zest and juice
1 tablespoon cardamom
½ tablespoon turmeric
½ cup fresh cilantro leaves
½ cup fresh mint leaves
2 large oranges, zest only
1 two-inch section fresh ginger root

Preparation:

Cut the tops off the pepper and discard. Cut the peppers into quarters. Place pieces into a food processor. Remove the skin off the ginger using a spoon. Cut the peeled ginger into smaller pieces and add to the food processor with the pepper. Pulse the food processor several times to lightly break up the larger pieces. Combine all the other ingredients except for the oil in the food processor. Pulse the processor until all of the ingredients are well chopped but not pureed.

Remove ingredients and place into bowl. Combine the oil with chopped ingredients using just enough to bind. Fill 2 one-quart mason jars half full and seal with the lid. Allow the curry to sit in the sun for 5 days. After being in the sun combine all of the ingredients into a blender and puree to a smooth consistency. Keep refrigerated until needed. Curry will keep refrigerated for 3 to 6 months.

turbot and salmon in a vanilla saffron broth

Yield: 4 servings

Ingredients:

Fish:
14 ounces of turbot filet, skin removed
14 ounces of salmon filet, skin removed
kosher salt
ground white pepper

Broth:
4 ounces leeks, julienne and reserve trimmings
4 ounces carrots, julienne and reserve trimmings
4 ounces celery, julienne and reserve trimmings
4 ounces green cabbage, julienne
1 small yellow onion, finely sliced and reserve trimmings
4 tablespoons butter
kosher salt
ground black pepper

1 Tahitian vanilla bean
1 large pinch saffron (If you have a digital scale measure 2 -3 grams.)
¼ cup dry white wine (Avoid the sweet white wines as they could make the broth overly sweet)

1 pound fingerling potatoes
½ cup extra virgin olive oil
1 teaspoon finely chopped garlic
kosher salt
ground black pepper

2 tablespoons finely chopped chives
1 tablespoon finely chopped fresh thyme

2 Roma tomatoes, skin and seeds removed and cut into ½-inch squares

Preparation:

Trim both fish filets into 1 ounce pieces, about 2 inches long and 1 inch wide depending on the thickness of the filet. Reserve the turbot scraps for a quick stock. Combine all the reserved vegetable trimmings with turbot scraps in a medium saucepan. Fill the pan half full with water and bring to a rapid simmer, just under a boil. Allow to simmer rapidly for roughly 20 minutes skimming away any impurities that rise to the surface. Soak saffron in white wine. Preheat the oven to 350 degrees.

Rinse the fingerling potatoes under cold water. Toss them in the olive oil, salt, and ground black pepper. Place on a half sheet tray or cookie sheet and roast in the oven for 10 minutes. Remove potatoes from the oven and toss with the chopped garlic. Return to oven and finish cooking the potatoes until they are fork tender.

Sweat the carrots, onion, celery, leeks, and cabbage in the butter until translucent not allowing them to color in any way. Season with salt and ground black pepper. Remove the saffron from the wine and add it to the sweating vegetables. (Rub the saffron vigorously between your fingers while you are adding it to the vegetables. This will help to release the flavors better.) Stir to coat the vegetables evenly and then add the white wine. Allow the wine to reduce slightly.

Strain the quick stock through a fine chinois or mesh sieve removing all the vegetable and fish scraps. Add to the vegetable and saffron. Allow the broth to simmer for 10 more minutes. Season the fish (both kinds) with salt and ground white pepper. Place the fish skin side down in a medium-sized saucepan. Strain the vegetables and saffron out of the broth with a fine chinois or mesh sieve. Cover and keep warm. Gently pour the broth (while it is still hot) over the fish. Finish cooking the fish over low heat (to a temperature of medium). Remove the fish from the broth. Cover and allow to rest. Strain any impurities from the broth and add the scraped vanilla beans and the empty pods. Over medium heat reduce the broth by ¼. Season to taste with salt. If needed, top with a little butter.

Remove the potatoes from the oven and allow to cool slightly. Slice the potatoes across into ¼-inch thick slices. Toss the slices with the chopped thyme and chives. Place the potato slices and julienne of vegetables on the center of a deep plate. Sprinkle the tomato pieces around the outside edge of the vegetables. Place the fish in an alternating stack on top of the vegetables and potatoes. Ladle the broth around the plate.

pan seared duck breast with almond potatoes and a vanilla raspberry sauce

Yield: 4 servings

Ingredients:

Duck:
2 large duck breasts
kosher salt
1 tablespoon ground black pepper
pinch ground cloves
pinch ground nutmeg
pinch ground allspice
pinch ground star anise
pinch pure ground vanilla
1 red delicious apple, cut into ½-inch cubes with the peel left on
1 pound fresh spinach, washed with leaves roughly cut up
1 fresh chopped shallot
2 tablespoons olive oil
1 pound small to medium whole new potatoes
¼ pound butter
1 teaspoon almond extract
1 teaspoon lemon juice
kosher salt

Sauce:
2 ounces chopped onion
1 ounce chopped carrot
1 ounce chopped celery
1 tablespoon olive oil
2/3 cup red wine
2 cups brown veal or beef stock
¼ cup raspberry vinegar
1 teaspoon pink peppercorns, soaked overnight in water
kosher salt
1 teaspoon vanilla extract
¼ cup heavy cream

Preparation:

Sauté onion, carrot, and celery in the olive oil in a saucepot. Allow the vegetables to start caramelizing. Season vegetables with salt and deglaze with the raspberry vinegar. Reduce vinegar until it is almost dry and then add the red wine. Allow the wine to reduce by 75%. Add the brown veal (or beef stock) and reduce the sauce at a simmer until has reduced by half of the original volume, about one hour.

Combine the ground black pepper, cloves, nutmeg, star anise, pure ground vanilla, and allspice, mixing well.

Score the fat side of the duck using a crossing pattern. Season the breast well with salt and the black pepper spice blend. Place a medium sized sauté pan over low heat and add the duck breast, fat side down first, and slowly render the fat from the breast. This will also crisp the ducks skin. Reserve the fat for the spinach and apples.

Place the potatoes in a deep pot and cover with water. Season the water lightly with salt and bring to a boil. Cook the potatoes until they are fork tender. Strain the vegetables from the reduced sauce. Discard the vegetables and put the strained sauce back into the sauce pot. Over low heat add the heavy cream, vanilla extract, and the pink peppercorns (first strain off water they have been soaking in). Allow the sauce to reduce and thicken over low heat. Do not allow to boil. Season to taste with salt.

Remove the rendered duck breast from the pan and pour off 90% of the excess fat. Return the pan to the stove top and increase the heat to medium high. Sear the other side of the duck and cook to the desired temperature. Medium rare is recommended. In a small saucepan brown the butter over high heat. Once butter has started to brown, remove from heat and carefully add the lemon juice and almond extract. Note: Do not do this over heat or an open flame as almond extract is highly flammable! Strain the potatoes from the water and return to the empty pot. Pour the butter sauce over the potatoes and coat evenly.

Using the excess duck fat, sauté the shallots in a medium-sized pan over medium heat allowing them to start caramelizing. Add the apples and heat through. Finally add the spinach and wilt it down completely. Season to taste with salt and ground black pepper.

Place the potatoes slightly above the center of the plate with a mound of the wilted spinach next to it. Thinly slice the duck and fan out one half breast on each plate. Spoon the sauce around. Do not allow it to touch any of the other elements. Fresh raspberries can be placed around the dish for garnish.

vanilla orange-mango pork chops

Preparation time: 25-30 minutes | Cook time: 2 hours | Yield: 5 servings

Ingredients:

5 medium-sized pork chops
3 tablespoons orange concentrate
2 cups water
1 tablespoon cornstarch
1 teaspoon vanilla extract
2 ½ tablespoons brown sugar
1 cup diced mango
2 tablespoon butter
salt
pepper

Preparation:

Pock the pork chops with a fork and season them with salt and pepper. Put aside. Combine the orange concentrate, water, and diced mango and blend together. Strain and add the brown sugar, vanilla extract, and cornstarch. Whisk together and set aside. Heat a large skillet and melt the butter at medium-high heat. Pan sear the pork chops approximately 10-15 minutes per side until they are golden brown on both sides. Remove the pork chops from the pan, put them in a plate and reduce the heat to low. Add the vanilla-orange-mango mixture into the skillet and whisk it to deglaze the pan. Add the pork chops. Cover and simmer for two hours.

braised sea bass with fennel

Yield: 4 servings

Ingredients:

2 pounds filets of fresh sea bass
kosher salt
ground white pepper
¼ cup vanilla olive oil

1/3 cup sliced shallots
2 fennel bulbs, large and roughly chopped, reserving 1 or 2 segments (large enough
for a small salad to sit in – 2 inches wide)
reserved fronds for garnish
½ cup of white wine
2 ounces (1/4 cup) butter
6 cups fish stock
6 cups chicken stock
kosher salt
12 sprigs fresh thyme
1 bay leaf
fennel sticks (fennel stalks, fronds (tops) removed
1 tomato, skin and seeds removed
1 tablespoon lemon juice
2 tablespoons of vanilla olive oil
kosher salt
ground black pepper
pure ground vanilla

Preparation:

Score the skin side of the fish with a crisscross pattern. Season well with salt and
ground white pepper and set aside. Preheat oven to 400 F(200 degrees C). In a deep
pan sweat the shallots and chopped fennel in a covered pan. Once the fennel and
shallots are translucent deglaze the pan with white wine and reduce the wine until it is
almost dry. Add the chicken and fish stocks to the pot and bring to a simmer.

In a large sauté pan heat the vanilla olive oil to medium high. Carefully add the sea
bass skin (side down). Allow the fish to obtain a good sear and start to caramelize on
the skin side. Once the fish is done on the skin side, remove from the pan and pat dry
with a paper towel.

Place the fennel sticks on top of the vegetables in the simmering broth. Place the
seared sea bass on top of the fennel sticks (bone side down this time). Cover the
pan with aluminum foil and place in the preheated oven to finish cooking the fish.
Cooking time will vary depending upon the thickness of the filet as well as the oven.
For a two-inch thick filet you will need to cook the fish for roughly 20 to 25 minutes.
In a small pot boil 2 cups of heavily salted water. Once water is boiling add to it the
reserved fennel (garnish). Blanch the fennel until it is fork tender. Cut into 4 equal
pieces.

Dice up the skinned and seeded tomato. Combine with the reserved fennel fronds, lemon juice, and vanilla olive oil. Season to taste with salt and ground black pepper. Spoon a nice bundle of salad into each of the four fennel segments. Remove fish from the pan cover and allow to rest. Strain out the rest of the ingredients reserving both the liquid and the vegetables and discarding the fennel sticks. Continue reducing the strained liquid over medium high heat adding the thyme sprigs and bay leaf. This is just to enhance the flavors – this liquid will not reach a sauce consistency.

Once the broth is ready, spoon a small mound of the braised fennel and shallots into the center of the plate. Place one piece of cooked fish over the top and garnish with the fennel tomato salad. Gently spoon the broth around the plate and finish off with a sprinkle of pure ground vanilla.

ground beef and pasta

Preparation: 15 minutes | Cook time: 40 minutes | Yield: 6 servings

Ingredients:

2 lbs ground beef
1 teaspoon dried thyme
¼ teaspoon garlic powder
½ teaspoon onion powder
2 tablespoons chicken bouillon
1 teaspoon sweet paprika
¼ teaspoon ground rosemary
¼ teaspoon ground sage
½ teaspoon dried parsley
2 vanilla beans cut lengthwise and scraped
1 teaspoon tomato paste
2 eight-ounce cans tomato sauce
salt
pepper
1-½ pounds of your favorite pasta

Preparation:

Mix ground beef, thyme, garlic powder, onion powder, chicken bouillon, paprika, ground rosemary, ground sage, and ground parsley. Season with salt and pepper. Brown the meat in a deep frying pan. Once the meat is thoroughly cooked, add the tomato paste, tomato sauce, and vanilla seeds (not the pods) and stir in with the meat. The vanilla beans in this recipe are not used for flavor; they help to cut the acidity of the tomato ingredients.

Simmer and stir regularly until the meat has the consistency of a "Sloppy Joe." Cook the pasta following the packaging instructions. Drain well and serve the meat on top.

mango glazed chicken breasts

Preparation time: 25 minutes | Cook time: 25 minutes | Yield: 6 servings

Ingredients:

6 boneless skinless chicken breasts
4 medium-sized mangoes
2 cups water
1 teaspoon vanilla extract
2 tablespoons brown sugar
1/8 dried thyme
1 teaspoon paprika
1/8 ground ginger
1 tablespoon melted butter
salt and pepper to season chicken

Preparation:

Preheat the oven to 400 degrees. Mix butter, dried thyme, paprika, and ginger in a small bowl and put aside. Season the chicken with salt pepper and ginger mixture. Let it cook for about 10 minutes. Peel mangoes. Slice off flesh and puree in blender with vanilla extract, brown sugar, and water. Strain and smear the chicken breasts with this sauce. Let cook for other 10 minutes. Smear the sauce all over the chicken breasts again and raise the temperature to 475 degrees. Bake 5 more minutes and remove.

shellfish trio in a vanilla mint citrus broth

Yield: 4 servings

Ingredients:

8 scallops (10-20 per lb.)
1 pound fresh mussels, cleaned
1 pound fresh cockles (clams can be substituted), cleaned
¼ cup vanilla vegetable oil
8 ounce (1 cup) onion, thinly sliced and cut into 2-inch pieces
4 ounces (1/2 cup) carrot, julienne
4 ounces (1/2 cup) leek, julienne
4 ounces (1/2 cup) roasted red pepper, julienne
2 fresh thyme sprigs
2 bay leaves
2 whole garlic cloves, green germ removed and thinly sliced
1 Tahitian vanilla bean, cut and scraped retaining both the pod and the scraped inner beans
1 cup white wine (preferably dry)
1 cup chicken stock
1 cup heavy cream
1 orange, juice and zest
1 lemon, juice and zest
kosher salt
ground white pepper
¼ cup fresh mint, thinly sliced

Preparation:

In a large bowl combine the mussels, cockles, onions, carrots, leeks, roasted red peppers, thyme, bay leaves, garlic, vanilla bean (pod and scraped beans), and the wine. Heat a large sauté pan with nothing in it on high heat. Once the pan is just about to smoke, carefully pour all the ingredients from the bowl into the hot pan. Cover the pan and allow the shellfish to cook until all are opened.

Remove the shellfish from the pan and add the chicken stock. Reduce the stock in half over medium heat. (Note: At this point a slight boil is acceptable.) Add the cream, orange juice and zest, and lemon juice and zest to the stock. Reduce the heat until the liquid is just simmering. Season to taste with salt and ground white pepper.

Remove and discard the empty vanilla pods, thyme sprigs, and bay leaves. Add the scallops and cook through (to about medium temperature). Just before serving add the cockles and mussels back to the broth and heat through. Season to taste. Garnish the soup with the thinly sliced mint and serve.

vanilla seared tilapia with shitake infused basmati rice and sautéed thai vegetables

Preparation time: 40 minutes | Cook time: 40 minutes | Yield: 4 servings

Ingredients:

4 eight-ounce tilapia filets
2 sprigs whole fresh thyme
1 tablespoon butter
1 tablespoon lemon juice
1 medium red bell pepper, julienne
1 small yellow onion, julienne
1 two-inch long fresh ginger toot, julienne
1 finely chopped clove garlic
1 cup basmati rice, rinsed
½ cup dried shitake mushrooms
½ cup vanilla oil
¼ cup chopped fresh mint
2 tablespoon chopped fresh thyme
2 tablespoon fresh parsley
salt and ground black pepper
4 six-inch long scallions, cut in half lengthwise

Preparation:

Bring 2 ½ cups water to a boil. Pour water over dried mushrooms. Cover and allow to sit for 15 minutes.

Strain off liquid from mushrooms and season well with salt and pepper. Add 2 cups of liquid to rice in a medium sized pan. Cover and bring to a boil. Once boiling, reduce the heat to low and allow rice to simmer until it is completely cooked. Chop the rehydrated mushrooms into pieces no larger than a quarter inch wide. Fold into the rice along with chopped mint, thyme, and parsley. Heat a large sauté pan on medium high heat with vanilla oil. Season tilapia filets with salt and pepper. Once oil is about to start smoking place the tilapia filets in the pan, bone side down.

Allow fish to sear completely on the bone side while basting the skin side with hot oil. Heat a second medium sauté pan to medium heat with vanilla oil. Once pan is hot add the ginger and onions. Allow both to start coloring then add the red bell peppers and the garlic. Season well with salt and pepper and cook the vegetables through. Turn the tilapia filets over and kill the heat. (Note: If you are cooking with a gas stove then just reduce the heat to low.) Add the two sprigs of fresh thyme, the tablespoon of butter, and tablespoon of lemon juice. Baste the fish continuously until the fish reaches a medium temperature. Remove fish from the pan and keep covered. Allow it to rest for five to eight minutes; then it is ready to serve.

salmon filet with ginger-vanilla butter

Preparation time: 15 minutes | Cook time: 2-3 minutes | Yield: 2 servings

Ingredients:

1 pound salmon filet
1/8 sweet paprika
1/8 onion powder
pinch garlic powder
dash dried thyme
salt and pepper to taste
1 tablespoon butter
fresh ginger, chopped
1 vanilla bean, split lengthwise and scraped

Preparation:

Heat a Teflon skillet to medium high. Spray with non-stick cooking oil. Season the salmon with salt, pepper, paprika, onion powder, garlic powder, and thyme. Place the salmon in the skillet with the skin side down first. Let it cook. Meanwhile, peel and finely chop the ginger and scrape the vanilla bean seeds. Set them aside.

Turn the salmon and cook the other side. Salmon cooks fast; approximately 1 minute per side.

Remove salmon from heat and melt the butter in a small pan. Add fresh ginger and vanilla bean seeds. Whisk until the ingredients are fully blended and pour on top of the salmon.

Note: If you have fresh tarragon, finely chop 1 leaf and add it to the ginger-vanilla butter.

smoked salmon parcels filled with avocado mousse and vanilla horseradish sauce

Yield: 4-6 servings

Ingredients:

1 pound smoked salmon cut into long slices (usually comes packaged this way)
½ pound fresh shrimp, preferably with the heads still on (if impossible only use ¼ pound headed shrimp)

Avocado Mousse:
2 ripe avocados
juice of ½ orange
juice of ½ lemon
kosher salt
ground black pepper

¼ cup French green beans, cut into finely chopped (1/8 inch squares) and blanched
¼ cup carrots, finely chopped and blanched
¼ cup celeriac, finely chopped and blanched

Note: Reserve all trimmings from cutting the vegetables and the liquid used to blanch them. Blanch the vegetables in lightly salted water.

Sauce:
1 ½ cups heavy cream
1 Tahitian vanilla bean, split and scraped
6 fresh thyme sprigs
1 teaspoon whole black peppercorns
1 bay leaf
¼ whole onion
2 cloves
salt and pepper
juice of 1 lemon
¼ cup fresh horseradish, grated

Garnish (optional):
salmon roe
fresh dill

Preparation:

Stud the onion with the cloves. Combine the cream, vanilla bean (both the scraped inside beans and the empty pod), thyme, bay leaf, and black peppercorns in a small pot and bring to a boil. Once the liquid boils immediately remove from the heat and allow to cool with all the ingredients still together.

In a medium-sized pot combine all of the vegetable trimmings and blanching liquid (add more water if needed). Poach the shrimp with the heads on until they are completely cooked. Remove the shrimp immediately and shock in ice water to prevent any further cooking.

Make sure all the shells are removed from the shrimp and then roughly chop. Make sure there are no pieces larger than ¼ inch. Carefully peel and remove the seed from the avocados. Smash the pulp and add the lemon juice and orange juice. Season with salt and ground black pepper to taste. Add the finely chopped vegetables to the avocado and mix well to combine. Add the chopped shrimp and mix well again. Adjust seasoning and the cover the mousse well so that there is no air in the bowl or able to touch the mousse. Air will cause the mousse to turn brown.

Strain the ingredients out of the cream discarding them and reserving the cream. Combine the cream with the grated horseradish and whisk to a soft peak. Add the lemon juice and season to taste with salt and ground black pepper. Lay slices of the smoked salmon out on a flat surface to create a 3 x 4 inch rectangle. Place 2 tablespoons of the avocado and shrimp mousse in the center of the rectangle and fold the edges around to enclose the mousse and create a uniform square parcel. Place 2 parcels per plate. Spoon the sauce over and around the parcels. Garnish with the salmon roe and fresh dill sprigs on top of each parcel.

Spinach And Mushroom Pizza

Preparation time: 20 minutes | Inactive time: 2 hours | Cook time: 25-30 minutes
Yield: 2 medium pizzas

Ingredients:

2 cups whole wheat flour
1 cup all purpose flour
pinch dried oregano
1 tablespoon yeast
1/3 cup vanilla herbed oil
1½ cups milk
3 pounds Kraft low-fat shredded mozzarella cheese
3 cups spinach
2 cups sliced baby portabella mushrooms
1 finely chopped large clove of garlic
Parmesan cheese to sprinkle
1 package Alfredo sauce
salt and pepper to taste

Preparation:

In a large bowl, mix whole wheat and all purpose flour, a pinch of salt, oregano, and the yeast. Add vanilla herbed oil and milk (if your milk is cold, put it into the microwave for 30 seconds before pouring it into the mixture). Knead until you have dough, about 10 minutes. Cover your dough with a kitchen towel and let it rest for about 2 hours until it is double in size.

Meanwhile, heat a large skillet at medium high. Pour 2 tablespoons of the vanilla herbed oil and chop onion, garlic, and mushrooms. Add these ingredients to your skillet. Chop the spinach. When the onions are clear, add the spinach and season with salt and pepper. Cook at high heat until the liquid from the spinach has evaporated and remove from heat.

Now make the Alfredo sauce according to the package instructions. Cover both your spinach and Alfredo sauce and let them rest. After two hours, preheat your over at 400 degrees. Check your dough and divide it into two bowls. Spray your pizza sheet with non-stick oil and spread the pizza dough all over the sheet. Pour half of Alfredo sauce onto the dough and spread out. Then sprinkle some of the low-fat mozzarella cheese. Take half of the spinach mixture and put it on top of the cheese. Sprinkle with Parmesan cheese and then sprinkle on the rest of the mozzarella cheese.

Take the other half of your dough and follow the same process on another pizza sheet. Bake both pizzas for 25 to 30 minutes. Remove from heat. Cut and serve immediately.

pork loin with plum compote

Preparation: 30 minutes | Cook time: 3 1/2 hours | Yield: 2 servings

Ingredients:

2 pork loins
salt
pepper
plum compote (recipe follows)
plum balsamic sauce (recipe follows)

Preparation:

Preheat the oven to 350 degrees. Season the pork loins with salt and pepper. Cover with foil and put into the oven for three hours. Take the pork loins out of the oven and brush the plum compote all over the loins twice. Put back in the oven at 400 degrees (uncovered) for 15 minutes. Remove the loin from the oven and brush the compote over it once more. Put it back into the oven for another 15 minutes. Remove loin from the oven and cover with foil to let it rest at least ten minutes before serving. Slice it into thin pieces and spoon the balsamic sauce on top.

plum compote:

Ingredients:

10 pitted plums
2 Tahitian vanilla beans, scraped
1 cup water
1 cup sugar
1 tablespoon light corn syrup

Preparation:

Chop the plums. Mix with the water, sugar, and corn syrup. Cut the vanilla beans lengthwise, scrape the seeds and the pods into the pot with the rest of the ingredients. When they are boiling, reduce heat to simmer. Let simmer for 25 minutes and remove the vanilla bean pods. Put aside.

plum balsamic sauce

Ingredients:

plum compote (leftover)
1 tablespoon butter
¼ cup balsamic vinegar

Preparation:

In a small deep saucepan melt butter and add the leftover plum compote and the balsamic vinegar. Stir until all ingredients are mixed well.

Note: The fruit compote and balsamic sauce can be made with apricots and peaches as well.

penne pasta casserole

Preparation time: 10 minutes | Cook time: 15-20 minutes | Yield: 6-8 servings

Ingredients:

½ pound penne pasta
1 lb ground beef
2 cloves garlic chopped
2 eight-ounce cans tomato sauce
2 13.5-ounce chicken broth
2 tablespoons chicken bouillon divided
½ teaspoon vanilla extract
1 chopped onion
2 stalks chopped celery
1½ cups chopped carrot
2 tablespoons herbed vanilla oil
chopped parsley
salt and pepper

Preparation:

Season the ground beef with 1 tablespoon chicken bouillon and your favorite meat seasoning. Brown in a large skillet on medium heat. When the meat is cooked, add the carrots, chopped garlic, and celery. In a medium bowl, mix the tomato sauce, chicken broth, the rest of the chicken bouillon, and the vanilla extract. Pour on top of the meat and stir. Add the uncooked penne pasta and re-season with salt and pepper to taste. The broth has to cover the pasta. Cover and let cook for approximately 12-15 minutes, stirring occasionally. The pasta should be al dente. Remove from heat and add the chopped parsley.

vanilla dry rub pork chops

Preparation time: 20 minutes | Cook time: 4 minutes | Yield: 2 servings

Ingredients:

4 boneless pork chops (about ¼ inch thick)
1 teaspoon salt
1 teaspoon sweet paprika
1 tablespoon brown sugar
1 vanilla bean split lengthwise
1/8 teaspoon black pepper
1/8 teaspoon dried thyme
1/2 teaspoon onion powder
1/4 teaspoon garlic powder
1/8 crushed coriander
¼ teaspoon ground cinnamon
1/8 teaspoon ground cloves
1/8 teaspoon ground allspice
2 tablespoons vegetable oil (preferably vanilla oil)

Preparation:

Place the pork chops in a glass container and set aside. Combine salt, paprika, brown sugar, black pepper, dried thyme, onion powder, garlic powder, ground cinnamon, cloves, coriander, and allspice in a small bowl. Split the vanilla bean lengthwise and scrape the seeds. Put the seeds on the meat and sprinkle it with the dry rub. Make sure the meat gets seasoned all over it by sprinkling on the dry rub two or three times.

Heat the oil in a large skillet at a medium high. Add the pork chops and let them cook about 2-3 minutes. Turn them over to cook the other side and turn the heat down to medium low. Add more oil if needed. Let cook for about 3-4 minutes or until the juices run clear. Since they are thin, they should cook fairly quickly. Remove from heat and serve warm.

For a complete meal you can combine this recipe with the elbow fennel pasta dish on the next page.

Note: The vanilla bean in this recipe is to enhance the sweet flavors of the dry rub ingredients.

elbow pasta with vanilla fennel

Preparation time: 15 minutes | Cook time: 20 minutes | Yield: 6-8 servings

Ingredients:

1 lb. uncooked elbow pasta
1 sliced onion
1 sliced fennel
1 garlic clove chopped
1 teaspoon vanilla extract
½ teaspoon crushed coriander
salt and pepper to taste
cherry tomatoes for garnish

Preparation:

Cook the pasta following package instructions. Remove the heart of the fennel and slice thinly. Save the fennel leaves for later. Heat a large skillet at medium high and sauté fennel, onion, and garlic. Add the vanilla extract and the crushed coriander. Season with salt and pepper.

Once the pasta has been cooked (approximately 17 minutes), remove from heat and drain well. Mix the pasta with the fennel. Re-season if needed. Serve on a large platter. Finely chop the fennel leaves and sprinkle all over the pasta. Garnish with the cherry tomatoes around the platter. Serve immediately.

Note: The vanilla extract in this recipe is used to enhance the natural sweetness of the fennel, onion, coriander, and garlic.

honduran fresh fruit compote

Please buy firm fruit to make this recipe. Soft fruit will become mushy.

Preparation time: 45 minutes | Cook time: 1 hour | Yield: 6 servings

Ingredients:

2 peeled and diced peaches
6 peeled apricots (pits removed)
2 peeled and diced mangos
2 peeled and diced plums
2 teaspoons lemon juice
3 sticks cinnamon
2 cloves
2 vanilla beans split lengthwise
1 star anise
6 whole allspice seeds
2 cups brown sugar
1 cup molasses
3 tablespoons light corn syrup
8 cups water

Preparation:

Add to a large deep pot of warm water the following: sugar, cinnamon, cloves, vanilla beans scraped and seeds, anise, allspice, molasses, and corn syrup. Let boil and add the fresh fruit coated with lemon juice to avoid oxidation. Cover, and reduce heat to simmer for about 1 hour.

Remove vanilla beans, anise, and cinnamon sticks. Let cool for a few hours and refrigerate.

honduran sweet tamales (montucas)

Preparation time: 2 hours | Cook time: 1 hour | Yield: 22 small tamales

Ingredients:

3 pounds boneless pork chops
1 pound frozen corn
3 cups maseca (corn flour)
3 sticks of butter
1 cup milk (half-and-half or buttermilk)
1 cup water
2 teaspoons ground cinnamon
1 tablespoon vanilla extract
1 cup of vanilla sugar (If you do not have vanilla sugar, you can use 1 vanilla bean per cup of sugar.)
pinch of salt
corn husks

Preparation:

Cut the pork chops into approximately one-inch pieces and season with your favorite meat seasoning. Brown in a medium skillet until they are fully cooked (about 12-15 minutes).

Put the corn husks into a large plastic bowl and pour hot water over them. Set aside. Thaw frozen corn and put it into the blender with the water. Strain it and mix it with the milk. Set aside.

In a medium bowl, mix the maseca with the salt, sugar, and ground cinnamon. Set aside.

In a deep pot, melt the butter at medium heat. Add the milk mixture and the vanilla extract. Turn the heat down to low/medium and add the maseca mix. Stir until the dough is thick and sticky, about 20 –30 minutes. Remove the pot from heat. Place the corn husks one at a time onto a flat surface and spoon the dough in the middle of the husk. Put a piece of pork on top, fold the sides in and then fold the ends up. Place in pressure cooker. If you do not have a pressure cooker, use your pasta pot.

Cover tamales and bring to a boil. Reduce heat to simmer and cook for an hour.

Note: Please do not use cornmeal as a substitute for the maseca corn flour.

scottish salmon baked in a vanilla rock salt crust with parsley cream sauce

Yield: 4-6 servings

Ingredients:

2 ½ pounds Scottish salmon filet (with skin) cut into 8-10 ounce portions
10 ounces rock salt
2 ¼ cups flour
3 egg whites
2 Madagascar vanilla beans, split and scraped reserving both the scraped inner beans and the empty pod
3 ounces clarified butter

Sauce:
1/3 cup white wine
2 chopped fresh shallots
1 ¼ cups fish stock
1 ½ cups heavy cream
1 teaspoon pure ground vanilla
5 ounces of fresh flat leaf parsley, roughly chopped
½ cup butter
kosher salt
ground white pepper

Garnish:
½ cup green lentils
3 ounces carrots, finely chopped
½ cup of bacon
kosher salt
ground black pepper
sherry vinegar to taste

1 sheet frozen puff pastry
1 whole egg for wash

Preparation:

Combine the rock salt, scraped vanilla beans, flour, egg whites, and clarified butter (melted) together in a bowl and mix well to combine evenly. It should look like a dry paste.

Preheat oven to 400 degrees.

Sweat the shallots in 1 tablespoon of butter until translucent. De-glaze the pan with the white wine and raise the heat to medium high. Reduce the wine until almost dry (about 75%) and then add the fish stock.

Allow the sauce to simmer and reduce by half (about 20 to 30 minutes). Put the lentils in a small saucepan and cover with 1½ cups of water. Season lightly with salt and bring to a simmer. Continue to simmer and stir occasionally until the lentils are cooked through.

Add the cream and continue reducing at a simmer for another 20 to 30 minutes. Render down the bacon in a small sauté pan. When the bacon is almost finished add the finely chopped carrot and allow to caramelize slightly.

On a sheet tray cover the each of the salmon fillets completely in the salt mixture ensuring there is no exposed flesh. Place in 400 degree oven and bake for 25 to 35 minutes (the salt crust should be hard to the touch and an internal thermometer should read 130 degrees F). Remove from the oven and allow salmon to start cooling in the salt crust. When about to serve remove the salt and any excess remains on the filet.

Roll out puff pastry on a lightly floured surface about ¼ to 1/3 inch thick. Cut into three-inch square portions and place on a greased sheet tray. Lightly brush with a beaten egg and bake at 400 degrees for 10 to 12 minutes or until golden brown and flaky.

Combine the lentils, rendered bacon, and carrots. Season to taste with sherry vinegar, salt, and ground black pepper. Finish the sauce by whisking in cold butter once the sauce is removed from the heat. Season to taste with salt and ground white pepper.

To serve, place a square of puff pastry in the center of the plate and generously spoon the lentils over the top allowing them to spill over the edge of the pastry. Place one portion of salmon on top of the lentils and pastry. Spoon the sauce around the plate almost like a soup. Garnish with the roughly chopped parsley.

noodle and vegetable stir fry

Preparation time: 20 minutes | Cook time: 15 minutes | Yield: 6-7 servings

Ingredients:

2 packages Ramen noodles (or cooked pasta)
6 cups water
2 cups chopped cabbage
1 ½ cups chopped baby carrots
1 chopped zucchini
2 cups chopped spinach
1 chopped onion
2 tablespoons oyster sauce
1 teaspoon vanilla extract
3 tablespoons herbed vanilla oil
Salt to taste

Preparation:

Put the noodles in a large microwave container with water and cook for 5 minutes. Drain well and put aside.

In a large skillet, heat the oil on medium high and add the noodles. Sauté the noodles for approximately five to seven minutes until they start to look golden brown. Add cabbage, onions, and carrots. Season the vegetables with the Ramen noodle seasoning and stir for about three minutes. Add the zucchini, spinach, oyster sauce and vanilla extract. Season with salt to taste. Stir for about three to five more minutes. The vegetables should be cooked tender, not mushy. Remove from heat and serve immediately.

honduran torrejas

Preparation time: 15 minutes | Cook time: 40 minutes | Yield: 20 torrejas

Ingredients:

4 egg whites
4 egg yolks
4 tablespoons pinol (See pinol recipe under Honduran Pinol.)
2 cups brown sugar
1 tablespoon corn syrup
1 star anise
6 seeds whole allspice
1 whole stick cinnamon
2 vanilla beans
4 cups water
vegetable oil for frying

Preparation:

In large deep pan boil the water with brown sugar, corn syrup, anise, allspice, cinnamon, and the vanilla beans (cut lengthwise and scraped). Reduce the heat to simmer and let cook for about 20 minutes.

In a frying pan, heat vegetable oil at medium heat.

Beat the egg whites at medium speed until they form hard peaks.   Add the egg yolks one by one without stopping your mixer. Add one tablespoon of pinol at a time and keep mixing. Once all of the ingredients are mixed, turn your mixer off. Spoon the mixture into your oil until it is golden brown. Remove from the fryer and let it sit on a plate with towel paper to absorb the oil. These fried balls are the torrejas.

Remove the vanilla bean, cinnamon stick, star anise, and whole allspice from syrup and put the torrejas in. Cover and let simmer until the syrup is thick. Serve torrejas warm or cold.

This dish is usually made for Easter or Christmas.

Note: You can substitute the pinol (vanilla-cocoa mix) for maseca (corn flour).

pan seared halibut with curried couscous salad and truffled white port vinaigrette

Yield: 4 servings

Ingredients:

Fish:

4-7 ounces halibut filets
kosher salt
ground white pepper
¼ cup olive oil
2 tablespoons butter
4 sprigs fresh thyme
1 ounce white port

Couscous Salad:

Soak 2 cups couscous in cold water until tender. (If using Israeli couscous only use 1 cup and do not soak in water before cooking.)
½ cup fresh mint eaves, pulled from stem and left whole
1 cup fresh spinach
1 small yellow onion, finely chopped
1 finely chopped garlic clove
1 tablespoon fresh parsley, roughly chopped
1 teaspoon fresh thyme, pulled from stem and roughly chopped
1 tablespoon yellow curry paste
2 tablespoons vanilla oil
kosher salt
ground black pepper

Vinaigrette:

375 ml. bottle of white port
¼ cup white truffle oil
1 tablespoon fresh cilantro, roughly chopped
1 tablespoon fresh shallots, roughly chopped
kosher salt
ground black pepper
1 bunch fresh watercress, large stalks removed
1 tablespoon lemon juice
1 tablespoon vanilla oil
kosher salt
ground black pepper

Preparation:

Reduce the white port over medium heat just above a simmer but not at a boil until reduced to only ½ to ¼ cup of liquid. Add the reduced port to the white truffle oil and whisk lightly to combine. Season with salt and pepper. Add the chopped cilantro and shallots, whisking again to combine.

Sweat (cook until soft) the onions and garlic for the couscous salad in the vanilla oil. Add the curry paste and couscous. Cook for a couple of minutes longer, stirring well to coat the couscous completely. Add to the couscous the mint, spinach, parsley, and thyme. Cook over medium heat until all the leaves have completely wilted. Season to taste with salt and black pepper. Heat the olive oil in a large sauté pan over medium high heat. Season the halibut with salt and white pepper.

Once the oil has come to temperature (just about to smoke) place the halibut fillets in the pan, bone side down. Baste the skin side of the fish with the oil while cooking. Allow the halibut to caramelize well on the bone side then flip the filets over and reduce the heat to low.

Add butter, thyme, and white port to the sauté pan and baste the fillets continuously until the filets have reached a temperature of medium. (The filets should just start to firm up but still be a bit fleshy in the middle.) Remove fish from the pan, cover, and allow to rest for 5 to 10 minutes. Dress the watercress with the vanilla oil and lemon juice. Season to taste with salt and ground black pepper.

Place the couscous salad in the center of the plate in a circular mound. Gently lay one filet of halibut on top of the couscous salad. Drizzle the truffle white port vinaigrette around the plate. Do not allow it to touch the fish or the salad. Garnish the halibut filet with the dressed watercress.

vanilla salmon gravalax

Ingredients:

    3 pounds fresh salmon filet (skin on if possible)
    6 ounces kosher salt
    4 ounces vanilla sugar
    2 tablespoons chopped fresh thyme
    1 tablespoon of chopped fresh cilantro
    3 Tahitian vanilla beans, split and scraped reserving only the inside beans
    1 bay leaf
    1 teaspoon coriander
    6 black peppercorns
    2 whole cloves
    2 whole allspice
    1 small whole star anise
    zest of 1 orange
    1 ounce Cointreau

Preparation:

Combine all the ingredients except salmon and Cointreau in a blender. Process until all of the herbs and spices have thoroughly combined and there are no large pieces remaining.

Coat the salmon in Cointreau, reserving half for later. Liberally cover the entire salmon filet in the salt mixture. Gently pour the rest of the Cointreau over the salmon without washing off any of the salt cure.

Wrap the filet tightly in cheesecloth without removing any of the salt cure. Cure the salmon in the refrigerator for three days.

Remove the salmon from the cheese cloth after three days and rinse off the salt cure. Slice the salmon as thinly as possible and enjoy.

salmon fettuccine with vanilla crème fraiche

Yield: 4-6 servings

Ingredients:

1 box fettuccine
kosher salt
4 to 6 filets of salmon, six ounces each
¼ cup extra virgin olive oil
4 to 6 sprigs fresh thyme
kosher salt
ground white pepper

Crème Fraiche: (made at least 24 hours in advance)
2 cups heavy cream
½ cup buttermilk
2 tablespoons pure ground vanilla
2 tablespoons chopped of fresh parsley
1 tablespoon chopped fresh thyme
½ tablespoon chopped fresh dill
kosher salt
ground black pepper
salmon roe

Preparation:

Combine the heavy cream and the buttermilk and whisk together well. Cover and allow the mixture to sit overnight at room temperature. If the mixture is thick the next day it is ready to use and can be stored in the refrigerator for up to 3 weeks. If the mixture is still very thin and runny, whisk again and allow to stand at room temperature for another day and then refrigerate.

Preheat the oven to 400. Coat the salmon filets liberally in the olive oil. Season well with salt and ground white pepper. Place on a sheet tray and lay one sprig of thyme on each. Bake for 15 to 20 minutes until they have reached the desired temperature (medium is recommended).

Cook the fettuccine noodles in boiling water until al dente. Strain the noodles from the water and place in a large saucepan. Toss the noodles in the crème fraiche over low heat until evenly coated. Add the pure ground vanilla, parsley, thyme, and dill. Stir the noodles to evenly disperse the herbs. Adjust seasoning with salt and ground black pepper.

Place one cup of the noodles in the center of a bowl. Rest one filet of baked salmon on top of the noodles. Garnish with salmon roe and serve.

pan seared scallops with coconut rice and candied red pepper and cilantro salad

Yield: 4 servings

Ingredients:

1 pound of U10 (10 or less in one pound) diver scallops
¼ cup grape seed oil
1 ounce butter
1 sprig fresh thyme
juice of 1 lime
kosher salt
ground white pepper

Rice:
½ cup jasmine rice
8 ounces coconut milk
1 tablespoon finely chopped fresh parsley
zest of 1 lime
kosher salt
1 dash Tabasco sauce

Salad:
1 red bell pepper – top, bottom and seeds removed, julienne
½ cup granulated sugar
½ cup water
kosher salt
¼ cup fresh cilantro, picked from stem
1 Asian pear, julienne
juice of 1 lime

Sauce:
8 ounces butter, cut into 1-ounce pieces
1 tablespoon water
1 Madagascar vanilla bean, cut and scraped
1 inch finely chopped fresh ginger root
kosher salt

Preparation:

Rinse rice in cold water. Combine with coconut milk in a sauce pot and season with salt. Cover and bring to a boil. Then reduce the heat to just over a simmer. Cook rice until tender. Finish seasoning with salt and Tabasco sauce. (Note: Tabasco in this recipe is not intended for heat. It is used to balance the acidity with the sweetness of the coconut milk.) Fold in the chopped parsley and the lime zest.

Combine sugar, water, and julienne of red bell peppers in a small sauce pan and bring to a boil. Once boiling, reduce heat to simmer and allow peppers to cook on simmer until tender and almost translucent.

When peppers are done drain off all liquid. (Reserve strained liquid as it makes a beautiful red pepper simple syrup.) While the peppers are still warm combine them with the pears, cilantro, and lime juice. Season to taste with salt.

In another small saucepan heat one tablespoon of water almost to a boil. Once the water is almost boiling remove from heat and quickly stir in the butter, one ounce at a time. If butter quits melting or starts to solidify briefly return to heat just to get the butter to start melting again. Once all butter is incorporated add the chopped ginger and vanilla beans. Season to taste with salt.

Season scallops with salt and white pepper. Heat grape seed oil in a large sauté pan on medium high heat. Pan sear scallops on one side until they have caramelized (just about medium rare). Turn scallops over in the pan and reduce the heat to low. Add the butter, fresh thyme, and lime juice. Continuously baste the scallops with the liquid in the pan until they have finished cooking (should start to feel firm to the touch).

Plate with rice down first and then the scallops slightly overlapping. Place the salad just on top of the scallops and the rice. Drizzle scallops with sauce and drizzle sauce around the plate just before serving.

8 : desserts :

Of course you can't talk about cooking with vanilla without talking about dessert! Vanilla enhances the flavor and sweetness of just about any dessert dish. Desserts tend to be everyone's favorite dish. Most people have come to know the taste and aroma of vanilla through the baked goods and sweets that our mothers made for us as children. I am no different. I love to make and then eat (sometimes a little too much) dessert.
So, let's dive in and have fun with vanilla and sugar. And what better way to start than with a simple Vanilla Bean Ice Cream?

simple no-cook vanilla bean ice cream

Preparation time: 3 minutes | Yield: 1 pint

Ingredients:

2 cups half-and-half
½ cup vanilla sugar
1 vanilla beans, split and scraped
½ teaspoon vanilla extract
½ teaspoon of salt

Preparation:

In a large bowl, combine the half-and-half, sugar, vanilla bean seeds, vanilla extract, and salt. Mix well. Add to an ice cream machine and process according to the manufacturer's directions.

candied tomato syrup

Makes 1 Pint

Ingredients:

6 Roma tomatoes cut into quarters
1 cup Karo syrup
½ cup vanilla sugar
1 cup water (for more tomato flavor use tomato juice instead)
12 sprigs fresh thyme
1 bay leaf
1 Tahitian vanilla bean, split and scraped reserving both the scraped pod and beans
kosher salt
ground black pepper

Preparation:

Combine all of the ingredients in a medium saucepan. Bring to a simmer, stirring slowly to dissolve the sugar and syrup. Allow the mixture to simmer slowly until it reaches the desired consistency (just a slight bit runnier than maple syrup).

Remove pan from the heat and allow to cool slightly. Process all of the ingredients in a blender. Strain the syrup through a fine strainer or cheesecloth. Serve cold or warm. This is great on the avocado ice cream.

patty's vanilla crème brulée

Preparation time: 5 minutes | Cook time: 40 minutes | Chilled time: 4 hours or overnight | Yield: 4 servings

Ingredients:

1/2 cup plus 2 tablespoons sugar
2 cups heavy cream
1 vanilla bean
1 teaspoon vanilla extract
4 egg yolks
2 tablespoons cornstarch
1 tablespoon butter
hot water

Preparation:

In a small bowl, whisk together the egg yolks.

In a small saucepan scald the cream, cornstarch, sugar, the vanilla bean (split in half), and vanilla extract. Do not allow the cream to boil. In a mixing bowl, whisk the egg yolks lightly and then drizzle in the warm cream, whisking to combine. Strain the cream mixture into six-ounce shallow buttered ramekins and place them into a small baking dish. Add enough hot water in the dish to reach halfway up the sides of the ramekins.

Bake the custards at 300 degrees in the middle of the oven until just set, 35 to 40 minutes. Carefully remove the ramekins from the water bath. Place plastic wrap on tops to avoid skin forming. Let them rest until they are at room temperature. Remove the plastic wrap and preheat the broiler. Sprinkle the sugar evenly over each of the crème brulee and caramelize with kitchen torch or use the oven broiler for 1 to 3 minutes.

Chill uncovered at least 4 to 5 hours or overnight.

sugar-free crumbly peanut butter cookies

Preparation time: 20 minutes | Cook time: 15 minutes | Yield: 20 cookies

Ingredients:

1 cup crunchy peanut butter
1 egg
¼ cup Splenda sugar substitute
1 tsp vanilla extract
1 tsp ground vanilla

Preparation:

Preheat the oven to 375 degrees. Mix all of the ingredients until the egg is well blended. Spoon the cookie dough onto the baking sheet. Make an "X" shape with a fork for decoration on the tops and bake for approximately 12-15 minutes.

rosemary vanilla ice cream

Makes 1 ½ to 2 Quarts

Ingredients:

4 sprigs fresh rosemary
4 Madagascar vanilla beans, split and scraped
1 cup fresh spinach
1 quart heavy cream
pinch kosher salt
4 egg yolks
½ cup sugar

Preparation:

Combine the rosemary, vanilla beans and scraped pods, salt, and heavy cream in a medium pot and bring to a boil. Remove from heat and allow to steep until cool to the touch.

Combine the sugar and egg yolks in a large bowl and whisk to a ribbon stage (yolks will be pale yellow and fluffy). Strain the rosemary and vanilla pods from the cream and bring the cream back up to almost a boiling point.

Combine the cream and spinach in a blender and blend until there are no visible pieces of leaf. Strain the cream again and slowly combine the hot cream with the sugar and egg mixture whisking continuously so the eggs do not cook. Return the mixture to low heat, stirring continuously until the mixture starts to thicken. Strain one last time and refrigerate overnight.

Process the mix in an ice cream machine until thick and almost frozen. Allow to freeze completely before serving.

vanilla soufflé omelet

Courtesy of Master Chef Annemarie Huste

Ingredients:

3 eggs, separated
3 tablespoons granulated sugar
½ tsp vanilla extract
½ vanilla bean, split and scraped
confectioners' sugar

Preparation:

Combine the egg yolks, 2 tablespoons of the sugar, the vanilla extract and vanilla bean (the scrapings). Beat until fluffy. Then beat the egg whites with the rest of the sugar until stiff. Melt the butter in a heavy omelets pan. Fold the egg-yolk mixture gently into the egg whites and pour into the pan. Cook over low heat for about 3 minutes, making sure the mixture does not stick to the sides of the pan. Then put the skillet under the broiler until the omelet puffs up and is golden brown. Slide the omelets onto a serving platter. Dust with confectioners' sugar and garnish with lemon slices.

vanilla bavarian cream

Courtesy of Master Chef Annemarie Huste

Yield: 8 servings

Ingredients:

2 cups milk
6 egg yolks
1 vanilla bean (split and scraped)
½ teaspoon vanilla extract
¾ cup sugar
1 ½ packages of gelatin
¼ cup cold water
1 cup heavy cream, whipped

Preparation:

In a heavy saucepan, scald the milk (heating it over low heat until just before boiling). Beat egg yolks, vanilla, and sugar until creamy. Pour the heated milk gradually into the egg mixture just to temper the eggs – you don't want to make scrambled eggs! Stir constantly. Cook mixture until it coats the back of a spoon. Remove from heat and add softened gelatin. Stir until dissolved.

Pour custard into a bowl and cool in the refrigerator until it just starts to thicken. Stir custard occasionally with a whisk to allow even cooling. When the custard is cool, fold in the whipped cream.

This cream can be used for topping on fresh fruits, cakes, pies, or any type of dessert.

brazilian fried bananas

Preparation time: 5 minutes | Cook time: 7 minutes | Yield: 6 chunks

Ingredients:

2 large ripe bananas (You should be able to still see the green in the peel)
1 large egg
1/8 teaspoon ground vanilla (or 1 vanilla bean scraped)
1 cup bread crumbs
1 teaspoon sugar
1/8 teaspoon ground cinnamon
Vegetable oil for frying

Preparation:

In a small bowl mix the bread crumbs, sugar, and ground vanilla. Put it aside. Preheat your fryer at 350 degrees. Peel the bananas and cut them in chunks of approximately two inches long. Whisk the egg in a small bowl and put the banana chunks, one by one, into it. Coat the bananas into bread crumb mixture making sure the chunk is all coated. Then coat the bananas again in the egg and back to the bread crumbs.

Put the banana pieces into the fryer. Turn them when the cooking side is golden brown. Remove from fryer when the chunks are golden brown all around. Sprinkle the banana with cinnamon while it is still hot.

yellow beet and vanilla sorbet
By Dan Caruso

Ingredients:

14 ounces yellow beets
1 tablespoon honey
1 cup simple syrup (equal parts sugar and water brought to a boil then cooled)
1 tablespoon lemon juice
2 Tahitian vanilla beans
2/3 cup Sprite

Preparation:

Peel the beets and cut them into ½-inch cubes. Blanch the beets in salted water until fork tender. Combine 1 cup of granulated sugar and 1 cup of water together in a saucepot and bring to a boil. Allow to cool before using.

Cut the vanilla beans lengthwise and scrape the beans from the pod. Reserve the pod to be used for vanilla sugar, salt, or vinegar. Combine the beets, scraped vanilla beans, simple syrup, lemon juice, and Sprite in a food processor.

Blend all the ingredients until smooth. Let rest overnight in the refrigerator. Process the cooled mixture in an ice cream machine until thick and almost frozen. Keep the sorbet in the freezer until needed for up to six months.

simple rice pudding

Preparation: 5 minutes | Cook time: 45 minutes | Yield: 2 servings

Ingredients:

5 cups whole milk
1 cup white rice
1 vanilla bean, split lengthwise
1 teaspoon vanilla extract
½ teaspoon ground cinnamon
1/2 cup vanilla sugar
1 tablespoon unsalted butter
fresh orange wedges for garnish

Preparation:

Combine the milk, rice, and butter in a heavy medium saucepan. Split and scrape in the seeds from the vanilla bean; add the bean, ground cinnamon, and vanilla extract.

Bring the milk to a boil. Reduce the heat to medium and simmer for about 25 minutes or until the rice is tender, stirring frequently. Mix in the sugar and discard the vanilla bean.

Cook about 30 minutes longer until the mixture thickens and the rice ends are open in both sides. Spoon the rice pudding into bowls. Place clear plastic wrap on top to avoid the formation of "milk skin." Refrigerate until cold.

cream cheese brownies

Ingredients:

½ cup (1 stick) unsalted butter
½ cup cocoa powder
1 cup all-purpose flour
½ baking powder
1/8 teaspoon fine salt
3 large eggs
4 ounces cream cheese (room temperature)
1 ½ cups sugar
2 vanilla beans cut lengthwise
1 teaspoon ground cinnamon

Preparation:

Preheat oven to 350 degrees. Beat the sugar, butter, cream cheese, and vanilla bean seeds until they are creamy. Add the eggs one at a time, beating after each addition until well blended. Please be careful not to over-mix the batter.

(cream cheese brownies, continued from page 133)

Use parchment paper in pan and spray it with non-stick oil. Pour in the batter into a 9 x13 baking pan. Bake for 30-35 minutes or until toothpick comes out dry. Cool the brownies in the pan on a rack.

To take the brownies out of the pan, lift the edges of the paper.   Cut the brownies into squares and serve.

pear upside down cake (with vanilla and ginger)

Yield: 6 to 8 servings

Ingredients:

1 sheet puff pastry
1/2 cup sugar
1/4 cup water
1 tablespoon light corn syrup
2 tablespoons unsalted butter
1 vanilla bean, split lengthwise, seeds scraped into small bowl
1 teaspoon grated fresh ginger
5 to 6 medium-sized firm pears (about 2 1/4 pounds), peeled, halved, cored, each half cut into 4 wedges and coated with lemon juice to prevent from turning brown

Simple No-Cook Vanilla Ice Cream

Preparation:

Roll out pastry on lightly floured surface until you can cut a 10" round. Pierce round all over with fork and then slide onto a baking sheet. Cover and chill the pastry for at least 24 hours.

Mix sugar, 1/4 cup water, and corn syrup in an ovenproof skillet over low heat until sugar dissolves. Increase heat and boil until sugar has caramelized and the resulting syrup is a nice dark amber color. This takes about 5 minutes. Remove from heat. Mix in the butter. When the butter has been incorporated add the vanilla bean seeds and ginger. Arrange pears overlapping in a circle in skillet. Place skillet over medium heat. Cook until pears are fork tender and the syrup has thickened enough to coat the back of a spoon. Place the hot skillet in an ice bath to cool the pears.

Preheat the oven to 375°F. Place the chilled puff pastry onto the top of the skillet, making sure that the pastry is inside the skillet and not hanging over the edges. Place skillet in the oven for 35 minutes or until the pastry is golden brown. Remove from oven and cool in the pan. This will take at least an hour.

To Serve: Reheat the oven to 375°F. Place the tart back into the oven for about 8 minutes. When the tart is removed from the oven, turn out onto a serving platter while still hot. Serve the tart with vanilla ice cream or whipped cream.

banana cream pie

Preparation time: 20 minutes | Cook time: 55 minutes
Yield: 5 servings per 1 pie shell

Ingredients:

Pie Shell:
½ cup flour
1 teaspoon baking powder
¼ teaspoon salt
½ cups rolled oats
½ teaspoon almond paste
1 cup brown sugar
¾ cup margarine, room temperature
1 teaspoon vanilla extract

Preparation:

Preheat oven to 375 degrees. Cream butter, almond paste, sugar, and vanilla extract. Add eggs one by one and mix well. Sift together flour, baking powder, and salt. Add to the wet mixture.

Spray pie baking dish with non-stick oil and pat mixture. Bake for 35 minutes or until browned. Let cool. This recipe will make two pie shells.

Cream:

Ingredients:

4 egg yolks
1 ½ cups heavy cream (or half-and-half)
1 vanilla bean, cut lengthwise
¾ cup sugar
2 tablespoons butter
3-4 tablespoons cornstarch
4 ripe bananas, sliced and separated
Whipped cream and vanilla powder for garnish

Preparation:

Melt butter in a big saucepan on medium low heat. Pour in heavy cream. Split and scrape in the vanilla bean. Put the seeds into saucepan along with the empty pods for additional flavor. Pour sugar and cornstarch and stir constantly. Slightly beat the egg yolks. Add some of the cream mixture to egg yolks to temper. Then add the egg yolks to cream mixture and stir constantly until thickened. Stir for 30 more seconds and remove from heat.

Spread first two sliced bananas on pie shell. Pour cream on top. Spread thoroughly and put on second half of bananas. Cover with foil and put into the refrigerator for a couple of hours to cool. Before serving put whipped cream on top and sprinkle with vanilla powder.

avocado and vanilla ice cream

Makes 2 ½ Quarts

Ingredients:

3 cups fresh avocado pulp, smashed
1 ½ tablespoon lemon juice
1 ½ tablespoon lime juice
2 Tahitian vanilla beans, split and scraped
3 cups whole milk
1 cup vanilla sugar
2 cups heavy cream
1 teaspoon kosher salt
3 tablespoons mild blue cheese at room temperature

Preparation:

Combine the avocado pulp, milk, sugar, salt, scraped vanilla beans, and blue cheese in a blender and puree the ingredients together until all the sugar is dissolved and there are no lumps of cheese. Put the puree into a large bowl and gradually whisk in the heavy cream. Once all of the cream is combined, whisk in the lemon and lime juices. Incorporate completely and adjust seasoning as necessary. Allow the mixture to chill completely in the refrigerator.

Process in an ice cream machine according to the manufacturer's instructions. Once processed, fill quart containers and allow the ice cream to completely freeze before serving.

baked floating cheese and vanilla soufflés

Yield: 4 servings

Ingredients:

4 egg yolks
2 tablespoons white wine
4 egg whites
3 ounces finely grated Parmesan Cheese
1 pinch cayenne pepper
kosher salt
ground black pepper
1 ¼ cups heavy cream
1 vanilla bean, split and scraped
10 sprigs fresh thyme
1 dried bay leaf
4 ounces grated Gruyere cheese
kosher salt
ground black pepper

Preparation:

Preheat the oven to 500 degrees. Combine the cream, vanilla bean (empty pod and inner scraped beans), fresh thyme, bay leaf, salt, and ground pepper in a small pot. Bring the cream to a boil. Immediately remove from the heat.

Strain the cream through a china cap removing the herbs and returning the hot cream to the pot. Add the grated Gruyere cheese to the cream. Over medium to low heat whisk the mixture until all the cheese is melted and the mixture is smooth. Adjust the seasoning.

Pour the cheese and cream into the base of an ovenproof pan. Allow to cool. Mixture should be ¼ to ½ inch deep.

vanilla bean flan

Ingredients:

1 1/4 cups milk
1 vanilla bean
½ tsp vanilla extract
1/4 cup sugar
salt
1 egg
1 egg yolk
1/4 cup sweetened condensed milk

4 ramekins

Preparation:

Preheat oven to 350°F. Heat the milk and vanilla bean (that has been split and scraped) into the milk, along with the vanilla pods in a saucepan over medium heat. Do not let boil! Remove from the heat. Cover and allow to set for about 20 minutes. Place sugar in a small skillet and allow the sugar to melt over medium heat. Stir until sugar is evenly dissolved and has caramelized (a deep golden brown color). Immediately pour into ramekins, covering the bottom of each. Set aside and allow to cool.

Mix together the whole egg, egg yolk, condensed milk, vanilla extract with a pinch of salt until smooth. Strain the milk and vanilla bean mixture to remove the vanilla pods. Gradually mix the milk into the egg mixture. Pour evenly into the ramekins. Place the ramekins in a cake pan. Place the cake pan/ramekins into the oven. When inside the oven, pour hot water into the cake pan until about halfway up the sides of the ramekins. Place a piece of foil over the cake pan and cook until the flan is set but not too firm. This should take about 35 to 40 minutes.

Remove from the oven. Remove the ramekins from the cake pan. Allow them to cool. Then chill them in the refrigerator at least 2 hours before serving. Remove the flan from the ramekins by running a paring knife around the edges to loosen the flan and then inverting onto serving plates.

Garnish with powdered sugar or caramel sauce.

yucca pie

Ingredients:

1/2 cup flour
1 cup sugar
2 cups grated yucca
2 sticks margarine or butter
2 cups coconut milk
2 tsp. baking powder
1 cup of cocoa powder
1 tsp. vanilla
1 vanilla bean
1/2 tsp. cinnamon
1/4 tsp. allspice
1/4 tsp. nutmeg
1/4 tsp. salt

Topping for pie:

1/2 stick of butter
1/2 cup brown sugar
½ cup flour
1 teaspoon almond paste
1 vanilla bean

Preparation:

Sift together flour, salt, and baking powder. Mix butter and sugar. Add vanilla extract, vanilla bean seeds, cinnamon, allspice, nutmeg, and coconut milk. Mix in dry ingredients. Pour into greased and floured baking pan. For the topping, melt butter in a small bowl and put aside. Mix sugar, flour, almond paste, and vanilla bean seeds. Add the butter and sprinkle the crumble crust on top. Bake at 375 degrees for approximately 45 minutes to 1 hour or until golden brown.

Don't know what to do with your ripe bananas? Try this.

triple vanilla banana pudding

Ingredients:

7 ripe bananas
1 cup sugar
1/3 cup vanilla oil
12 slices of wheat sandwich bread
1 teaspoon vanilla extract
1 teaspoon ground vanilla
4 eggs
1 cup milk
pinch of salt

Preparation:

Preheat the oven to 350 degrees. Peel, cut, and mash the bananas in a large mixing bowl. Add the eggs, sugar, vanilla extract, ground vanilla, oil, and milk. Cut the bread slices into cubes and soak them in the banana mix. Pour into greased large Pyrex dish and cook for one hour or until a toothpick inserted comes out clean.

Remove from heat and let cool. When mixture reaches room temperature, put into the refrigerator for at least 4 to 5 hours, or overnight.

Note: If you do not have ground vanilla, use two vanilla beans.

grandma's cake donuts

Ingredients:

1 cup sugar
1 cup milk
4 tablespoons Crisco
2 eggs
3 cups flour (separated), plus more for kneading.
4 tsp baking powder
½ tsp salt
1 tsp ground vanilla
1 tsp vanilla extract
Vegetable oil for frying

Preparation:

Mix all of the wet ingredients in a mixer, except milk. Mix dry ingredients (only two cups of flour) and add them to the wet ingredients little by little, alternating with the milk.

The dough will be a little runny. Flour a flat surface and knead the dough adding the third cup of flour until the dough is no longer sticky but still very soft.

Roll dough out to ½ inch thick and cut with donut cutter.

Pour oil into a frying pan or a large skillet and heat to 375 degrees. Carefully add the donuts and turn them until both sides are golden brown. Remove from the oil and let them cool on a rack for about 15 minutes. Enjoy!

Note: If you do not have ground vanilla, use 1 vanilla bean.

about Arizona Vanilla Company

Arizona Vanilla Company was started by Patty Elsberry in order to have relatively inexpensive, but high quality vanilla at her disposal. In her search for good supplies of quality vanilla, she found that there was a business opportunity to offer these same high quality beans to the rest of the world. So, Arizona Vanilla Company was born.

Arizona Vanilla Company is dedicated to finding the highest quality vanilla beans and vanilla products, at the most competitive prices. Arizona Vanilla is in a relentless pursuit of those two goals.